A Humanist in Africa

Letters to Colin M. Morris

from

KENNETH D. KAUNDA
President of Zambia

Abingdon Press

NASHVILLE   •   NEW YORK

A HUMANIST IN AFRICA

Copyright © Kenneth D. Kaunda and Colin M. Morris 1966

Published in Great Britain by Longmans, Green and Co., Ltd.

Library of Congress Catalog Card Number: 68-11713

PRINTED AND BOUND BY THE PARTHENON PRESS, AT
NASHVILLE, TENNESSEE, UNITED STATES OF AMERICA

Contents

Introduction

No man, claimed Madame Cornuel, is a hero to his valet. Certainly no man is a Superman to his close friends, who are privileged to see him in his braces, as it were, stripped of the shining armour of his public presence, the 'warts and all' rather more prominent on his relaxed countenance than when he is all stiffened up for public scrutiny. I have known Kenneth Kaunda as a nationalist on the run from the police, as a restrictee in the bleak detention camp at Kabompo, struggling for his political life as he contended with Harry Nkumbula for the leadership of the African people, as a political opponent and as President of the Republic of Zambia. I have often seen him 'in his braces', far out of range of the cheering crowd and the probing camera, in a variety of moods and in some very strange places. I have had ample opportunity to do what every ordinary citizen has the right to do but rarely gets the chance—to take the measure of the man who holds one's destiny and the destiny of a whole nation in his hands.

Let me declare, in honesty, my interest. I am an admirer, quite unashamed and not a little sentimental, of Kenneth Kaunda. And if this brief assessment of him smacks of sycophancy then I can only claim that what some may regard as immoderate praise I would term accurate description. There is a distressing tendency in the modern world for a public personality to get less than his due from his friends because they are afraid of being called toadies. It is often left to those who know him least to assess his quality. But it seems to me that where one is in a position to testify to the goodness of a man whose character is of vital interest to millions then one should shout one's discovery from the house-tops, and the Devil with the detractors!

As a Christian minister, embroiled by force of circumstances in the politics of Central Africa over the past ten years, it is a matter of peculiar concern to me to be able to give the lie to the popular sneer that politics is a dirty game. What does true morality in politics look like? Is it possible to handle power without being tainted by it? What kind of character can go down into the morass of compromises, accommodations, conflicts, alliances and betrayals that are characteristic of political life and still emerge with his integrity intact and his hands clean?

My knowledge of Kenneth Kaunda has taught me that there is an affirmative answer to be returned to such questions for he operates according to a rigidity of moral principle which could well be cold and repulsive if it were not shot through with great humanity. It is not easy to take one's stand openly for morality in politics without appearing priggish or Olympian. It is possibly Kenneth Kaunda's greatest attribute that he has shown that goodness can be attractive.

And strong-principled he most certainly is! Take his refusal to eat meat. Here is a man who once saw a group of African women being man-handled outside a white-owned butcher's shop because they were protesting against the exorbitant price of meat. There and then he swore that he would never again eat what they had been unable to afford. Nor has he done, as many a hostess has discovered to her distress: her elaborately prepared meat course goes untasted. He is endlessly apologetic, but quite inflexible. For him a principle is once and for all, and he must testify to it not by pious prating but personal sacrifice. He imposes his abstention on no one else nor does he make it a public issue. It is his quiet, personal witness; his way of identifying himself with even the minor sufferings of others. It is symptomatic of the Gandhian streak in his character, which has the effect, though this is not the intention, of shaming people into changing their behaviour patterns where no amount of coercion would succeed.

Mahatma Gandhi has had many admirers amongst African nationalist leaders, some of whom have paid lip-service to his philosophy of non-violence whilst their followers, uncommitted by their leaders' quirks, have engaged in mayhem on the boundaries of the movement. Indeed, it was a time-honoured tactic for nationalists, publicly committed to passive resistance, to demand concessions from a colonial government on the grounds that their followers, whom they were privately encouraging, were getting out of hand. Kenneth Kaunda, on the other hand, not only declared his allegiance to the philosophy of non-violence but rigidly enjoined it upon his followers to the point where his leadership teetered in the balance.

Non-violence is all very well provided it meets with a positive response from those authorities against whom it is directed. But nationalists, not unnaturally, tire of turning the other cheek when they are on the receiving end of vigorous action by the Police and Army who are not committed to any policy of non-violence. The men of violent passions in a nationalist movement can claim with some justification that it is only when the shooting starts that the Government is disposed to take their demands seriously. For months on end, the freedom struggle in Zambia hung fire whilst Kaunda waited to see what response his passive resistance campaign would evoke from the British Government. Furious debates raged within the party and demands were clamant for a degree of violent action to demonstrate that the African people meant business. But such was Kaunda's moral ascendancy over his followers that most of his colleagues, who in private confessed to having no faith whatever in passive resistance as a political tactic, swallowed their impatience, kept their tempers and held the restive rank and file in check.

Some great leaders have waded to power through the spilt blood of their followers. That Zambia's freedom struggle was virtually bloodless is testimony both to Kenneth Kaunda's example and to his powers of persuasion. But he might well have been repudiated as a man of peace out of place on the battlefield. One thing is sure. Had he been faced with a straight choice between abandoning his policy of non-violence or relinquishing the leadership of his Party, he would today be a private citizen of Zambia, teaching in a village school or tilling a plot of land. For him, there is no compromise on the moral principle once he has committed himself to it.

Take the case of corruption in public office, a scourge of many new nations. Kaunda dismissed two Cabinet Ministers for irregularities in dealing with a company which had contractual arrangements with their Ministries. As far as an ordinary member of the public, without private sources of information, can gather, the offence was little more than a departure from a long-standing convention. Yet they had to go. Both were his personal friends. One had fought by his side in the freedom struggle and was a most valuable party official. Political expediency indicated the smoothing over of the whole business at a time when the public announcement of their dismissal would put into the hands of Mr Ian Smith's Government valuable ammunition to be used in the propaganda war being waged between Rhodesia and free Africa. But they had to go. Kaunda had assured the people of Zambia that nothing short of the highest standard of integrity in public servants would be tolerated. The decision could not have been made without pain for Kaunda is a kind man. There is nothing about him of a Macmillan who could, without warning, dismiss half his Cabinet in an afternoon and emerge as urbane as ever, not a hair out of place.

Kenneth Kaunda's kindness is sometimes described by observers of the political scene as an irremediable weakness in a nationalist leader who, they claim, must have a streak of iron in his character. I am not so sure that the righteous anger of a kind man is not more fearsome a quality than political ruthlessness. Certainly, neither considerations of personal friendship nor political expediency will deter him from a tough course of action when his principles are challenged.

Kaunda is an intensely religious man. Hard-bitten reporters have been heard to complain that at every one of public meetings they are treated to a sermon complete with Biblical references before he gets down to the hard news. It is fashionable for most national leaders to invoke the Almighty, if only to demonstrate that they are prepared to take second place to Someone, who, mercifully, is not in the running for their particular office. Kaunda's faith works itself out in personal obedience. Daily Bible reading and prayer are his invariable rule. There is an atmosphere pleasantly redolent of Victorian times about his family life. He loves a hymn singing session around the piano not because the tunes of the hymns are catchy but because their words bespeak his own experience—for one gift bequeathed to him by his father, the Rev David Kaunda, is a faith, simple, strong and unshakeable.

The theologian might describe him as a syncretist— someone concerned to bridge the gap between different religions and to incorporate into his experience the best elements of them all. Though impatient of labels, Kaunda describes himself in the following pages as a Christian humanist but he can make himself at home in a cathedral, mosque, temple or synagogue with an ease that makes nonsense of religious divisions. Zambia is a secular State, not because its President undervalues the Christian contribution to national life, but because he sees his nation as a meeting ground not only of many races but also of many religions. He is one of the country's greatest impetuses towards the reunion of the Christian Church because he steadfastly refuses to take seriously denominational differences.

But those who fondly imagine that religious fervour and political naïvety go hand in hand should conjure with the complexity of the problems which have faced Dr Kaunda since he assumed the Presidency of the Republic of Zambia. The economy of the state is abjectly dependent upon copper, which in turn requires a large expatriate community to provide the technical and professional skills to exploit it. An inherited history of racial antagonism has led to a situation where, in the sharply defined spectrum of colour, to be trusted by one racial group is, by definition, to excite the suspicion of the other. Yet the toughest white copper-miner will confess, however grudgingly, that he is prepared to remain in Zambia so long as 'that chap Kaunda remains in power'. He is able to perform the feat of instilling some degree of security in the white community without alienating the support of the black masses who have put him in power. The secret is neither in propaganda nor in double talk but in a quality of transparent sincerity which even the bitterest racist recognises.

Nothing has taxed Kenneth Kaunda's diplomatic gifts so severely as Zambia's ambiguous situation caused by the accidents of geography whereby she is politically committed to the free North whilst remaining economically linked with the white South. South Africa and Rhodesia, besides providing many of Zambia's vital supplies, control her major channels of communication. Kaunda has, therefore, been unable to indulge in the luxury of extravagant condemnation and sabre-rattling threats characteristic of some States to his North, comfortably remote from any direct encounter with the white-dominated nations at the Southern tip of the

Continent. Yet his standing in Pan-African circles remains high and no doubt is cast upon the sincerity of his desire to help free the millions of Africans still suffering political repression.

Mr Ian Smith's Unilateral Declaration of Independence on 11th November, 1965, presented Kaunda's government with a crucial challenge and let loose an avalanche of economic, political and diplomatic consequences which would have daunted a government with fifty times the experience of Kaunda's one-year old administration. Kaunda's cool nerves, together with the exercise of that rarest of all gifts in a politician—knowing when to keep silent regardless of provocation—kept down the temperature and so avoided a conflagration which would have laid Zambia waste, economically. And yet the whole world knew where Kaunda stood on the Rhodesian issue. Nor did Zambia's perilous economic situation render him amenable to blackmail. Mr Ian Smith's threat to impose an exorbitant royalty on all Wankie coal exported to Zambia was met by Kaunda's firm refusal to pay even though the power supply to Zambia's copper mines was imperilled. This was one of those 'stand and fight' situations where, as a matter of principle, Kaunda would not back down at any cost.

The inside story of the ramifications of the U.D.I. issue may never be fully known, but when the historians are in a position to draw some general conclusions Kenneth Kaunda's tight-rope-walking feat between Pan-African demands, British vacillation, and internal restiveness will certainly be regarded as an outstanding diplomatic performance by any standards.

It is a great pity that since the seventeenth century the word 'peasant' has had attached to it a derogatory flavour implying crudity, unsophistication and gullibility. For in the best sense of the word, Kenneth Kaunda has a peasant mentality—a quality he shares with Abraham Lincoln. He is a man of the people with his roots firmly in the ground, not ashamed to confess his humble origins and exhibiting a rough-hewn wisdom which is rarer than any intellectual gift. There is about him the traditional courtesy of the old Africa. He defers to his elders, however unlettered, and has a cavalier respect for women. He can merge into the life of the village as easily as he moves in international diplomatic circles. This ability is a consequence of his humanist philosophy. There is only one standard of valuation of all human beings. He refuses to make false choices between the sophisticated and the primitive, the intellectual and the peasant. He wears the trappings of power almost with an air of apology for fear that they might cut him off from ordinary people.

Many national leaders inspire awe, respect and even fear. Kenneth Kaunda is widely loved. He is 'Ken' to hundreds of people though none of them would dare to presume upon this intimacy where his Presidential dignity is concerned. He has his enemies but tends to talk of the most inveterate of them in a tone of amused affection which neutralises them more effectively than any amount of bitter invective.

He has his shortcomings and has made his mistakes. When a critical biography is written, possibly some of the superlatives will be toned down and these apparently absolute judgements modified. But I am certainly not the man to carry out that critical enquiry. I do not believe that there is so much goodness abroad in this world that we can afford to deride it. In my view, for what it is worth, Kenneth Kaunda is a good man whom power has not corrupted and who is the exponent of a humanism in politics which may be Zambia's most precious gift to Africa.

*   *   *

For a number of years, Dr Kaunda and I have kept going a running debate by letter, discussion and memorandum on a whole range of topics. It is from this mountain of material that I have selected the contents of this book. I must plead guilty to a certain degree of literary licence in describing the excerpts as 'letters'. The bulk of Dr Kaunda's views have been contained in a pile of blue Minute Papers with which he has bombarded me from time to time.

But I have insisted on retaining the word 'letters' in the sub-title because it conveys the correct impression of immediacy and spontaneity. It would be unfair to Dr Kaunda to give any impression that he at any point sat down and wrote a considered treatise on the subjects covered in succeeding papers. These are his thoughts on the march, dictated in haste, linked by me in chapter form and amplified where necessary by personal discussion.

My concern has not been to select his views on matters of immediate topical interest because I have learned by bitter experience that what is topical in Africa as a manuscript leaves the typewriter is likely to be a matter of history by the time the printer gets his hands on it. I have attempted to illustrate the thought processes and philosophy of life of one of Africa's outstanding personalities. In this way, I hope that the book will retain a certain abiding interest for being unrelated to the transience of today's headlines.

Colin M. Morris
Chingola,
Zambia

A HUMANIST IN AFRICA

I

A Humanist in Africa

Having thought over our discussion of the other evening, I feel that it might be useful to attempt to put into words my philosophy of life. It seems to me that when the people place great power in a leader's hands they have a right to know the code of values in terms of which he will exercise it. But I am no armchair philosopher. The whole of my adult life has been taken up with the freedom struggle in Africa. The political arena rather than the library has been my workplace. All my thinking has been done on the march except for a period when I had a certain amount of time for reflection whilst a guest of Her Majesty in some of the best prisons in Central Africa!

I suppose I could be called a humanist, though I have never had the leisure to read the standard works on the subject. I have a passionate belief in the worth and possibilities of man and I expect him some day to achieve perfection. By perfection I do not mean sinlessness. But for all his weaknesses, man is growing in self-knowledge and will one day fully realise his capabilities. He is painfully thrusting his way forward and must eventually evolve social, political and economic institutions to which he will be completely adjusted, and within which his vices will be neutralised and his virtues strengthened.

The book by Teilhard de Chardin* which you sent me seems to support my contention, and I am grateful to you for putting me in touch with his thought. Of course, Teilhard de Chardin's vista is much broader than my own, taking in as it does the very origins of the universe, but I am not being facetious when I claim that what he has discovered as a philosopher I can testify to as a politician. For in spite of all the hard things that are said about my profession, the experienced politician is a student of Man and, if he is to survive, must be an acute social observer. There has been a kind of telescoping of time on the African Continent so that this progressive movement of mankind onwards and upwards can be clearly traced. Though nationalism has been the vehicle of this advance, its power-sources lies deep within the nature of Man himself.

Our brethren in Malawi took as their slogan for the freedom struggle the Cinyanja word 'Kwacha!', which means 'Wake up, the dawn is here!' But awaken to what? Teilhard de Chardin puts it well when he speaks of Man's 'growing capacity to situate himself in space and time to the point of becoming conscious of his place and responsibility in relation to the Universe'. I would like to claim that phrase as the philosophical basis of nationalism. To 'situate oneself in space and time' is surely to discover one's identity, which was beaten out of shape by the impact of Colonialism, and to 'become conscious of place and responsibility in relation to the Universe' speaks of the dignity and stature of Man. He must measure himself not against the rest of the animal world, nor in terms of the little fragment of local history through which he has lived, but against the Universe itself.

I believe that a great humanist revolution is sweeping Africa at the present time. Apparently, the late nineteenth century—the Imperialist Era—was also the hey-day of humanism in Europe. I have no doubt that many imperialists thought that their invasion of Africa was a humanist gesture

* *The Future of Man* (New York: Harper, 1964).

—to liberate the poor benighted heathen trapped within the barbaric tribal system. At least that is what they claimed in their biographies. In fact, Colonialism, for all its benefits, devalued Man. It created élite societies in which men's worth was determined by an irrelevant biological detail— skin pigmentation. And even more serious, the colonialists set out to destroy our self-confidence. They dinned into the African mind the idea that we were primitive, backward and degraded, and but for their presence amongst us, would be living like animals. The result is that even today in an inde-pendent African State you will find a certain sector of the population suffering from a *Bwana* complex. They cannot stand on their own feet as free men but must look over their shoulder all the time for the approval of the White Man.

It was nationalism, of course, which restored our self-confidence, for it taught us what we could do together as men, and only as men—at no stage in the freedom struggle had we the material power or military might of the colonial-ists. It was humanity in revolt that won us our freedom. I believed we triumphed not because we had the greater power, but because we occupied the superior moral position. This fact, enlightened colonial powers such as Britain recognised, and could no longer rule us without forfeiting their self-respect. When I came away from London in 1964 with Zambia's Independence Constitution in my brief case, I and my colleagues were greeted at Lusaka Airport by a huge cheering crowd and in that most moving moment it struck me afresh that it was *people* who had done this thing. It was the triumph of a Man-centred society over a Power-centred society.

This intense belief in the possibilities of Man is a dis-covery which Africa appears to be making long after the West has discarded it. We in Africa look in amazement and disappointment at the two great Power Blocs flirting with global destruction in order to build up the ego of their peoples. It is our recurrent nightmare that we might be sucked into this conflict and have our people robbed of life at the beginning of a bright new day for Africa.

To a certain extent, we in Africa have always had a gift for enjoying Man for himself. It is at the heart of our traditional culture, but now we see the possibility of extending the scale of our discovery by example to the whole world. Let the West have its Technology and Asia its Mysticism! Africa's gift to world culture must be in the realm of Human Relationships. The Colonialists may talk condescendingly about the things they have taught us, yet I honestly believe that we have been all the time much nearer to the heart of the things that really matter than our Western teachers. After all, don't the scientists tell us that Africa was the cradle of Man? The way things are going, Africa may be the last place where Man can still be Man.

To talk in such terms is to be branded a naïve idealist and visiting politicians are sometimes at pains to point out that my optimism will not survive the hard realities of power politics as Zambia takes her place in the community of free nations. Maybe so, but it is surely better to start off with high hopes and struggle to realise them than to adopt the defeatism and cynicism which is miscalled realism in those nations that preach endlessly about human freedom and yet have multiplied power to the point where the Man it is intended to serve has become irrelevant.

*   *   *

You ask me to expand my statement that Africa may be the last place where Man can still be Man. I think that two elements have gone to make up what might be called the African philosophy of Man. These are the African's relationship with Nature and the psychological impact upon him of centuries of existence within tribal society.

I believe that the Universe is basically good and that throughout it great forces are at work striving to bring about a greater unity of all living things. It is through co-operation with these forces that Man will achieve all of which he is capable. Those people who are dependent upon and live in closest relationship with Nature are most conscious of the operation of these forces: the pulse of their lives beats in harmony with the pulse of the Universe. They may be simple and unlettered people and their physical horizons may be strictly limited, yet I believe that they inhabit a larger world than the sophisticated Westerner who has magnified his physical senses through invented gadgets at the price, all too often, of cutting out the dimension of the spiritual.

Only the other evening I was reading in the Book of Psalms. I came across a verse in which the Psalmist is praising God for having 'set his feet in a large room'. Now David came from a pastoral people dependent upon Nature, and though I find some of his ideas about God crude and mistaken there is a sort of bold sweep to his thinking which comes from inhabiting the 'large room' of Nature rather than the machine-packed work-shop of industrial society. The Psalmist can make a declaration linking God and the Universe in one verse of fifty words. Scientifically-orientated modern Man often requires a hundred thousand words to state a thesis concerning some tiny, specialised aspect of truth. Now I know, of course, that these two approaches are not contradictory and I am not denying the importance of the scientific method. But my point is that people in close relationship with Nature are forced to ask *big* questions however crude their answers might be. I could entertain you for hours retelling the traditional stories of my people I first heard in my childhood, many of which offer ingenious if somewhat fanciful explanations of the great riddles of life to which the world's great thinkers have sought solutions.

It is easy, of course, to romanticise Nature, but this is an error more likely to be made by those comfortably protected from it than people like myself who have experienced its cruellest moods in disease, blight, famine and drought. To be exposed to Nature and to have to live your life at its rhythm develops humility as a human characteristic rather than arrogance. Men are more companionable and take the trouble to live harmoniously together because they know that only by acting together can they reap the benefits and try to overcome the hardships of Nature.

Was it not the Luddites in England who went around smashing the new machines of the Industrial Revolution because they could not face the future? I am no Luddite! I welcome all the advantages which Western science and technology have brought to Africa. I even welcome the fact that technology reduces our dependence upon the uncertainties of Nature, in spite of all that I have said. Yet my question is this. Is there any way that my people can have the blessings of technology without being eaten away by materialism and losing the spiritual dimension from their lives? I suppose the answer is that however intensely we industrialise, the vast majority of the peoples of Africa will still live in close contact with Nature and so keep alive this element in our culture.

The second element in African humanism stems from the structure of the traditional society and its effects upon African psychology. The devoted work of anthropologists has now borne fruit and only the bigot would dismiss tribal society as primitive and chaotic. It is widely recognised that these societies were, in fact, highly organised and delicately balanced in the network of relationships which held their members together. I need not go into great detail since the characteristics of the tribal community are well known. Let me draw attention only to three key factors which reinforce the humanist outlook.

The tribal community was a *mutual* society. It was organised to satisfy the basic human needs of all its members and, therefore, individualism was discouraged. Most resources such as land and cattle might be communally owned and administered by chiefs and village headmen for the benefit of everyone. If, for example, a villager required a new hut, all the men would turn to and cut the trees to erect the frame and bring grass for thatching. The women might be responsible for making the mud-plaster for the walls and two or three of them would undoubtedly brew some beer so that all the workers would be refreshed after a hot but satisfying day's work. In the same spirit, the able-bodied would accept responsibility for tending and harvesting the gardens of the sick and infirm.

Human need was the supreme criterion of behaviour. The hungry stranger, could, without penalty, enter the garden of a village and take, say, a bunch of bananas or a mealie cob to satisfy his hunger. His action only became theft if he took more than was necessary to satisfy his needs. For then he was depriving others.

Obviously, social harmony was a vital necessity in such a community where almost every activity was a matter of team work. Hence, chiefs and tribal elders had an important judicial and reconciliatory function. They adjudicated between conflicting parties, admonished the quarrelsome and anti-social and took whatever action was necessary to strengthen the fabric of social life. I should emphasise that this way of life was not a kind of idealised social experiment such as may be found in Europe where groups of people take themselves off into pleasant rural surroundings in order to avoid the tensions of industrial society. Life in the bush is hard and dangerous and a high degree of social cohesion is necessary for survival. The basic unit of life is not the individual or immediate family (as in industrial societies) but the community. This means that there must be fundamental agreement upon goals and all must act together.

In the second place, the tribal community was an *accepting* community. It did not take account of failure in an absolute sense. The slow, the inept and incapable were accepted as a valid element in community life provided they were socially amenable. Social qualities weighed much heavier in the balance than individual achievement. The success-failure complex seems to me to be a disease of the age of individualism—the result of a society conditioned by the diploma, the examination and the selection procedure. In the best tribal society people were valued not for what they could achieve but because they were *there*. Their contribution, however limited, to the material welfare of the village was acceptable, but it was their *presence* not their *achievement* which was appreciated.

Take, for instance, the traditional Africa attitude to old people. I remember being horrified on the first occasion I made the acquaintance of that Western phenomenon, the Old People's Home. The idea that the State or some voluntary agency should care for the aged was anathema to me, for it almost seems to imply that old people are a nuisance who must be kept out of the way so that children can live their lives unhampered by their presence. In traditional societies, old people are venerated and it is regarded as a privilege to look after them. Their counsel is sought on many matters and however infirm they might be they have a valued and constructive role to play in teaching and instructing their grandchildren. Indeed, to deny a grandparent the joy of the company of his grandchildren is a heinous sin. The fact that old people can no longer work, or are not alert as they used to be, or even have developed the handicaps of senility in no way affects our regard for them. We cannot do enough to repay them for all they have done for us. They are embodied wisdom; living symbols of our continuity with the past.

No doubt a defender of the Western way of life might retort that institutions for the care of old people are inevitable in large-scale societies and that but for the efforts of the State and voluntary agencies many old people would starve. This is undoubtedly true but it merely serves to underline my point that in a society which regards person to person relationships as supremely important no one can be so isolated that responsibility for his welfare cannot be determined and assigned.

The experts have all kinds of standards by which they judge the degree of civilisation of a people. My own test is this. How does that society treat its old people, and, indeed, all its members who are not useful and productive in the narrowest sense? Judged by this standard, the so-called advanced societies have a lot to learn which the so-called backward societies could teach them.

In the third place, the tribal community was an *inclusive* society. By this I mean that the web of relationships which involved some degree of mutual responsibility was widely spread. I would describe industrial society as an *exclusive* society because its members' responsibilities are often confined to the immediate family, and I have noted that the family circle may be a self-entire little universe, preventing the acceptance of wider commitments.

Let me give you an example of the inclusiveness of the traditional society. I do not restrict the title 'father' to my male parent. I also address my father's brothers as 'father'. And I call my mother's sisters 'mother' also. Only my father's sisters would I address as 'aunt' and my mother's brothers as 'uncle'. My 'brothers' would include not only the male children of my father but also certain cousins and even members of the same clan who have no blood relationship to me at all. Now this, to the Western mind, very confusing state of affairs, is not merely a matter of terminology. These are not just courtesy titles. With the title 'father' for example, goes all the responsibility of parenthood and in return all my 'fathers' receive my filial devotion. Hence, no child in a traditional society is likely to be orphaned. Should his literal parents die then others automatically assume the responsibility for his upbringing. By the same token, no old person is likely to end his days outside a family circle. If his own offspring cannot care for him then other 'children' will accept the duty and privilege.

The extended family system constitutes a social security scheme which has the advantage of following the natural pattern of personal relationships rather than being the responsibility of an institution. It also provides for richness in knowledge and experience for those fortunate enough to be part of it. Granted, I have been describing the characteristics of small-scale societies and it could be argued that such a system would not work where hundreds of thousands of people are gathered together in cities and towns. But the attitudes to human beings which I have set out are not solely a function of social organisation. They are now part of the African psychology. I am deeply concerned that this high valuation of Man and respect for human dignity which is a legacy of our tradition should not be lost in the new Africa. However 'modern' and 'advanced' in a Western sense the new nations of Africa may become, we are fiercely determined that this humanism will not be obscured. African society has always been Man-centred. We intend that it will remain so.

*   *   *

You question my use of the term 'African psychology'. If I may say so, there is a naïve kind of liberalism about in Africa which waxes sentimental about multi-racialism and is terrified of admitting to any difference between the races lest this be interpreted as racial arrogance. I do not see why we cannot admit to racial differences, and even glory in them, without this observable fact being given a moral connotation in terms of 'superiority' and 'inferiority'. After all, one's enjoyment of the bursts of colour in a beautiful garden does not depend upon one's ability to ignore the fact that the rose is different from the carnation and that each bloom makes its distinctive contribution to the whole effect.

Possibly 'psychology' is not the appropriate word, but I do believe that there is a distinctively African way of looking at things, of problem-solving and indeed of thinking—we have our own logic-system which makes sense to us however confusing it might be to the Westerner. If I were, from my own observation, to try to summarise the difference between African and Western psychology I would say that the Westerner has a problem-solving mind whilst the African has a situation-experiencing mind. The Westerner has an aggressive mentality. When he sees a problem he will not rest until he has formulated some solution to it. He cannot live with contradictory ideas in his mind; he must settle for one or the other or else evolve a third idea which harmonises or reconciles the other two. And he is rigorously scientific in rejecting solutions for which there is no basis in logic. He draws a sharp line between the natural and the supernatural, the rational and the non-rational, and more often than not, he dismisses the supernatural and non-rational as superstition. He brings his problem-solving mind to bear upon the Miracles of Christ, or the strange happenings we call witchcraft, and twists himself in knots trying to find rational explanations which will not need to take account of supernatural forces.

Africans, being a pre-scientific people, do not recognise any conceptual cleavage between the natural and the supernatural. They experience a situation rather than face a problem. By this I mean they allow both rational and non-rational elements to make an impact upon them, and any action they may take could be described more as a response of the total personality to the situation than the result of some mental exercise. I think too, that the African can hold contradictory ideas in fruitful tension within his mind without any sense of incongruity and he will act on the basis of the one which seems most appropriate to the particular situation. Every missionary is aware of the African Christian of some maturity who in one situation will behave as his Faith has taught him and in another follow the practices of traditional religion, or even combine the two, as for example, in death rituals. I suppose the standard retort would be that he has not yet been fully 'converted' to Christianity and that vestiges of paganism still remain in his mind. It is not as simple as this. The African mind does not find it easy to think in terms of Either-Or. It is open to influences which make Both-And seem desirable. This attitude comes, I think, from the sense, which I mentioned earlier, of inhabiting a large world in which there is no partition between the natural and the super-natural.

Some people will claim that all I am saying is that the African people are still primitive and need education in order to learn to think as the Westerner thinks. This I decisively reject. Nor do I believe it necessary that our people must make an Either-Or choice between these systems of thought. There are obviously areas of activity where the problem-solving approach is the only sensible one. There is not an African and European way of balancing the Budget or splitting the atom. There is only a right way and a wrong way. The laws of Science and of Economics must be obeyed, and where the time element is vital, the techniques of the scientific method must inevitably be used. But in the field of human relationships, which is my primary concern, I would submit that the African approach may be both profoundly right and more humane. It certainly avoids the danger of treating people as things.

This is not just theory. Every day of my life I face the necessity of making difficult and important decisions. The techniques of administration and decision-taking are fairly standard the whole world over. But often I am conscious of an extra dimension to a problem which preoccupies me to such an extent that a European civil servant standing at my shoulder awaiting my decision may feel that I am prevaricating on a matter which seems open and shut to him. I am not infallible; sometimes I am right and sometimes wrong. But even when I am wrong, I believe that my people will understand because we are along the same wavelength of thought. I have consciously tried to think through the problem in an African way, even though there is no shortage of well-meaning observers giving me good advice as to the obvious solution according to some Western textbook.

Does all this mean that the modern African leader is a split personality caught between two ways of thought, always in a state of tension—a sort of walking civil war between the Western and African elements in his nature? Inevitably so; yet it is amazing how one can learn to live with this tension and even count it as an asset adding to the wealth of one's personality. One of the discoveries we are making about Man in Africa is just how adaptable he can become and how his nature can expand to measure itself against the magnitude of the challenges which face him. The split I fear is not that between the Western and African elements of my personality but that between heart and head. It is possible to be right in a problem-solving sense and yet betray one's integrity. The danger of the scientific method is that it is an imperialist! It invades and attempts to dominate areas of life where it has no right to be. Because it opens so many doors, it is fatally easy to regard it as a universal passkey which will fit any lock. Through its blessings expressed in technology and science, the peoples of Africa can undoubtedly become more prosperous, clever and efficient. But will it make them more sociable, charitable and responsible? I believe the source of these social virtues lies already deep within our own culture.

*   *   *

Our discussion on African and European ways of thinking has set me pondering about the African character. Though I have always been aware of certain qualities which Africans seem to have in abundance, I have never tried before to catalogue them. So let me sing you a hymn in praise of my people!

First on the list I would place the African's enjoyment of people for their own sake. Our love of conversation is a good example of this. We will talk for hours with any stranger who crosses our path, and by the time we part there will be little we do not know about each other. We do not regard it as an impertinence or an invasion of our privacy for someone to ask us 'personal' questions, nor have we any compunction about questioning others in like manner. We are open to the interest of other people. Our curiosity does not stem from a desire to interfere in someone else's business but is an expression of our belief that we are all wrapped up together in this bundle of life and therefore a bond already exists between myself and a stranger before we open our mouths to speak.

This characteristic of ours can easily be misunderstood. You may remember a little while ago there was a minor scandal when one of my colleagues who had been booked to appear on television in Kitwe did not arrive for the programme. It turned out that on his way to the Lusaka Airport, he caught sight of three men by the roadside, one of whom he had known as a boy. Good manners required that he should greet them so he stopped his car and was soon engaged in animated conversation. Only the sound of the Viscount roaring over his head reminded him that he ought to have been on the aeroplane. Now the Western critic might view this incident as irresponsibility or dereliction of duty. He might further claim that this Minister would best have shown his love for the people by fulfilling his television engagement. Nevertheless, it is the besetting temptation of a public servant to be concerned only for people in the abstract and insulate himself from contact with people in particular. I would doubt the genuineness of the love for people of any leader who did not show it in an openness to the claims of specific persons he encountered.

Colonial civil servants have been known to fume with impatience because a never-ending procession of people streams through the office of an African Minister, many of them apparently with no purpose other than to say 'Hello!' The well-meaning civil servant would claim that these social calls prevent the Minister from getting on with his work. But these people *are* the Minister's work. For us, to talk of ourselves as the 'servants' of the people is more than a political platitude. It is a precious part of our culture and tradition. The essence of servanthood is surely availability, openness to the demands of all those who have a claim upon one's services. This seems to be in a marked contrast to the Western tradition of leadership. The symbol of rank in Western society appears to be unavailability. The more important you are, the more difficult it is for anyone to get access to you unless they are important too. In our tradition, to be known by name to others is to 'belong' to them in a very real sense, and therefore the more widely you are known the greater the number of people of all kinds who have the right of access to you. Hence, I do not find it odd if a humble Zambian, unknown to me, takes it into his head to call at State House and greet me. He and I are brothers and to spurn him would be a sin as great as shutting myself off from my own family.

Naturally, some compromise must be achieved between the claims of particular persons and of the people in general or else Government could not function. But this exposure of Ministers to casual encounter with the people they are pledged to serve ensures that they do not become soulless machines, answerable for their actions and policies only at election times. It is more important to us that Government should be humane than efficient.

We are also a patient people. This quality has developed because of our dependence upon Nature. You cannot hurry the sunrise, the rains and the harvest. Having adapted ourselves from time immemorial to the rhythm of the natural world, we are not given to fretting and fuming when things do not happen at the press of a switch or the turn of a wheel.

If we cannot achieve a goal immediately, we do not write off as time wasted the intervening period. We are content to *be*. There are an infinite number of things to see, think about and talk over. We cannot understand this Western urge for ever increasing speed which seems to be accompanied by an inability to know what to do with the time saved. Where living is concerned, style is more important to us than pace.

Insensitive critics often mistake our patience for indolence and dumb passivity. Like the Colonialists of the past, the Rhodesian and South African Governments are making the fatal error of mis-reading the patience of their African peoples as lack of any strong feeling about their policies. Deep beneath the apparently placid surface powerful forces are building up. These patient people await only a sign that the due time has come, then they will act in unmistakable manner. It is possible to trespass upon the patience of the African people for too long. This fact lends urgency to the work of the governments of independent African States. Our people will not be content to be deprived of their human rights and the material blessings to which they are entitled indefinitely. Their patience must not be viewed as lack of concern.

We are also a forgiving people. If this were not the case, the lot of Europeans in modern Africa would be very unpleasant indeed. But it is not in our nature to bear grudges and to exact revenge. Many Europeans have spoken to me in wonderment at the smoothness of transition to majority rule and the total absence of major racial incidents. For us the past exists only as a moral and a lesson, purged of emotion. Having suffered from the brutal generalisations of racist thinking, we have only one standard of valuation— individual merit. No European is expected to pay for the sins of his compatriots. Provided he is prepared to accept us as we are, we are happy to return the compliment.

When I talk of our people being a forgiving people I do not mean that they are morally superior or more religious than other peoples. In our eyes, forgiveness is a social virtue which implies much more than words of absolution. It involves restoration to fellowship, the re-establishment of links which have been severed by the past behaviour of the one who needs to be forgiven. Because the only life we have known is life-in-community, to be unforgiven is to remain outside the circle of relationship and this state of affairs is socially undesirable, quite apart from the cruelty of the punishment. For the rogue individual is a threat to our peace and harmony. He must be brought back into the fellowship so that the community is once again complete and united against all outside threats. We cannot allow overweening pride and the desire for revenge to rule our hearts because these vices are destructive of community. Our whole life is togetherness and to be cut off from our fellow human beings is to die in the soul.

Much has been written and recorded of our love of rhythm. We are renowned for our laughter, music and dancing. Rhythm is the very expression of the life-force within us; it is the illumination of our spirit. It is symbolic both of our relationship with other people and with all created things. This strong rhythmic pulse beats throughout all our culture. In speech, we make no clear-cut distinction between prose and poetry. Our utterance is rich in proverb and artistry of expression is as important as the communication of meaning. The idea of solo performance in music is foreign to us. It is an intolerable strain to sit passively in a concert hall and be played or sung to. In spite of ourselves, our whole body responds to a musical beat; we cannot resist swaying our heads, shuffling our feet and clicking our fingers.

The pulse of life beats strongly within us. Our laughter, music and dancing are an expression of grace. We are glad to be alive and are thankful that we have been preserved from natural hazards (and some unnatural ones) such as disease, wild animals, slave-traders, conquering armies and colonial oppression. Every important event in the life of the village and all the major milestones of our personal lives are commemorated by ceremonials which include music and dancing. And it is at such times that the barrier between the natural and the supernatural crashes down. We are conscious of only one world—living generations sway in rhythm with gods and ancestral spirits. Even the devoutest Christian is likely to have second thoughts at times such as these!

The unsympathetic observer uses this aspect of our lives to prove the case that we are an easy-going people who do not take life seriously. He does not see deeply enough into us. We take life seriously, all right, but we steadfastly refuse to take ourselves seriously. Even the victims of circumstance, such as the poor and unemployed, can always summon a smile and, if given half a chance, do a little dance. This is not irresponsibility, it is gratitude. Whatever they do not possess, they do possess the gift of life itself and this is compensation for much that is denied them.

Allied to this sense of rhythm is our optimism. Africans are great optimists; they have a sunny outlook and hate gloom and pessimism. This is why a humanist outlook accords well with our temperament whilst grim Marxism and the narrow Christianity which preaches endlessly about the depravation of Man do not. The source of our optimism is not the ability to ignore unpalatable facts and refuse to look steadfastly upon the dark side of life. Our optimism springs rather from our faith in people. The nationalist leaders in particular learned the lesson during the freedom struggle that whatever demand we made upon our people, they rose to answer it. Nothing deterred them from achieving their goal. Ordinary people did extraordinary things. I can afford to be an optimist when I recall with thankfulness the tremendous achievements of the people of Zambia. Whenever we faced an obstacle to the fulfilment of our aims, from somewhere in our movement a man or group of men would emerge who were able to overcome it.

I find it difficult sometimes to keep my temper when well-meaning observers commiserate with me that I must run a country with so few trained personnel. They invariably manage to imply that it is tragic that political expediency has forced me to 'Africanise'—replace seasoned and experienced expatriates with inexperienced young Zambians—as though I were implementing a policy of despair. What the critics fail to realise is that these so-called inexperienced young men have often packed more into their short lives than many senior expatriates. Scarcely out of their teens, they have planned, suffered, fought and won through. They have helped to organise and discipline a mass movement numbering millions, handled hundreds of thousands of pounds, travelled, spoken and written tirelessly. What they lack in formal training for government, they more than compensate for in dedication. Why should I not have confidence in them? I *know* them as a soldier knows his comrade in the heat of battle.

We are optimists because our prayers have been answered; our trust in God and our fellow men has not been betrayed. We refuse to fall victim to the philosophy of realism which is the next thing to despair—a philosophy which expects men to fail and therefore paralyses their initiative.

To dwell as I have done upon the strengths of the African character is not in any sense to deny that it also has its weaknesses, but I do not see that we are going to build the society of our dreams by dwelling morbidly upon our failures and weaknesses. Our attitude is that we shall do better next time. I would rather expect too much of my people and be let down occasionally than become a cynic who is never disappointed because he expects the minimum of the people with whom he must deal. He may not suffer disillusionment but neither will he be able to inspire people by his example.

It is faith in the goodness of people that we must reinstate in Africa. Though it is a hard thing to say to you of all people.

I believe that the legacy of certain types of Christianity which emphasise the sinfulness and depravity of Man is more of a curse than a blessing to us. I doubt that the people of Africa really knew what misery was until the missionary came. Do not misunderstand me, I do not mean that they were never sad, cast down and reeling before life's blows. But they never made the cult of misery a way of life which is what bad religion taught them. A people who have had their self-confidence driven out of them by aggressive Colonialism need a faith which strengthens their belief in their own possibilities, not one which has them grovelling before an Old Testament God, beating their breasts and wailing about their unworthiness.

We have also seen something of the very best Christianity, thank God; I myself have benefited from it and so I am unlikely to make the mistake of condemning the Christian contribution out of hand. Yet I cannot help feeling that the secret of the growing impact of Islam upon Africa is that it is a religion which reinforces men's belief in themselves without denying their dependence upon Allah. It is a militant, nationalistic, intolerant faith, yet it is a faith for men. Is Christianity a faith for men?

*   *   *

I wonder whether, after my last outburst, you are planning to strike me off the roll of members of the United Church of Zambia! I hope not, because I want to reassure you of the Christian basis of my humanism. I have carefully studied the definition of humanism given by Mr H. J. Blackham in his Introduction to the symposium, *Objections to Humanism*.* He claims that 'there is no supreme exemplar of humanist ethics, because, on humanist assumptions, there is no *summum bonum*, no chief end of all action, no far-off crowning event to which all things move and for which all

---

* (Philadelphia: Lippincott, 1965).

things exist, no teleology, no definitive human nature even'. I am certainly not a humanist in Mr Blackham's sense if this quotation describes the basis of the humanist case. I must be a Christian humanist!

By Christian humanism, I mean that we discover all that is worth knowing about God through our fellow men and unconditional service of our fellow men is the purest form of the service of God. I believe that Man must be the servant of a vision which is bigger than himself; that his path is illumined by God's revelation and that when he shows love towards his fellow men, he is sharing the very life of God, who is Love. When Man learns, by bitter experience if in no other way, that the only hope for the peace and happiness of the world is to give political and economic expression to love for others we shall have entered not the Kingdom of Man but the Kingdom of God.

For all my optimism about Man's possibilities, I do not make the mistake of forgetting that he is God's creature, with all that this means both in limitation and in dignity. Nor do I deny the reality of sin. The besetting sin of the humanist is Pride. The significance of Jesus Christ is surely that He spells death to our pride by showing us how far short of God's design for us we are. He is the Man against whom all men must measure themselves when they try to live the life of love. Then they will discover that He lived the perfect life of love not by His own unaided ability but because He was totally submissive and obedient to the Will of God.

I do not believe that we were intended to thrash our way blindly through history, either as individuals or as nations. Every act of obedience to God must take us nearer to some great goal. Only God knows what the great blueprint of life is, and the most that we can do is always be ready for God to cross our path and lead us off in some strange, new direction.

Since I was a small child I have been conscious of God's guidance. As a shy and somewhat retiring person, I could never have willed myself to take a prominent part in the independence struggle, nor even now presume to hold high office in Zambia, did I not believe that it is God's Will for me that I should.

These are my convictions and I try to live by them. Those who wish to may scoff, but I would remind them that these are the convictions not of a religious professional but a practising politician, and politics is not noted as a trade which breeds sentimentality and idealism. But this is the tale of my years and the fruit of my experience.

I... a very long poem in praise of
Ma... ...dren learn it by heart. Our
discussio... ...y conviction that only the
recovery of a s... ...lity of Man will get politics
back on the right track. How can we teach our people to
appreciate the preciousness and dignity of Man in a world
where we have been conditioned to think in terms of millions
and thousands; where we can shrug off the news that ten
thousand people have died in an earthquake or even one
hundred in an air crash with a momentary wince of regret
and a feeling of relief that the earthquake occurred somewhere else and we were not travelling on the aeroplane?
How can we humanise our politics in Zambia so that the
humblest and least well endowed of our citizens occupies a
central place in Government's concern? The point of
departure must surely be to look afresh at Man—not Man
for anything or Man *as* anything but Man in himself—and
sing his praises unashamedly. For until every person learns
self-valuation, it is pointless trying to humanise Government
and other great institutions within which Man tends to be
submerged. If a person has no self-appreciation how can
he expect others to treat him as he deserves? By self-
appreciation I do not, of course, mean pride or conceit but
rather a realistic recognition both of one's possibilities and

limitations. Such an exercise is an essential prelude to any new thinking on political policy in which we may engage.

Let me try to put my thoughts about the nature of Man into some kind of order.

Man is an animal. The fact that he shares the same ancestry as lower forms of life is not something of which we need be ashamed. It makes his achievements all the more impressive that they emanate from a being who is as susceptible as other forms of life to natural hazards—heat and cold, hunger and thirst, disease and so on. Indeed, Man is less well equipped than most other animals for the battle of survival. Is it not amazing what this frail creature has achieved by using his mind and imagination in place of lost instincts? Yet it is tragic that having created or invented all kinds of protections against natural hazards, his greatest hazard is his neighbour. The most dangerous threats both to his survival and his progress come from the failure of his social instincts, his inability to live in community and to make his highest faculty, love, the law of his being.

But every time Man is confronted with a decision he finds himself at a crossroads. The choice is between rejoining his animal ancestors and struggling against his lower self in order to achieve spiritual freedom. There is a price to be paid either way. To align oneself with the animal world is to sacrifice dignity for comfort. To choose human freedom is to purify one's spirit through suffering and sacrifice. And by every decision he makes, Man shows whether he belongs to the past or the future; whether he is a biological dead-end or a new departure in evolution, thrusting upwards into the realm of the Spirit.

Reading the works of Teilhard de Chardin I am exhilarated by the majestic vision he unfolds of a Universe, all of whose component parts are moving toward some great goal. Such a picture is both comforting and challenging: comforting, because it means that there is after all a point and purpose in life, there are great forces at work with which we can co-operate; and challenging because we are encouraged to be better than our best to speed along this process whereby Man is thrusting like an underground seed upwards toward the light.

I suppose that Man is evolving now in his mind rather than through his physical make-up. It would be foolish to claim that we are wiser or better in a moral sense than were our ancestors of hundreds of years ago, yet I do believe that we understand more about ourselves and our place in the Universe. And we can trace the evolution of our conscience even through the legal structure of our society. We no longer regard slavery, the subordination of women, child labour and racial discrimination as either inevitable or desirable. I hope that in the not too distant future the evolution of our conscience will take us to the point where we recognise War as the wasteful and degrading thing that it is and a totally irrelevant solution to our problem.

Within the mind of Man, the evolutionary process has been speeded up immeasurably. I suppose it took the creatures we call birds hundreds of thousands of years to evolve to the point where they could fly. Man has solved this problem in half a century! Granted, every new area of discovery produces a new set of problems; the greater the circle of light, the larger the surrounding area of darkness. And the most difficult of these problems are those concerned with social living. Yet just as we evolved Plato, Beethoven, Shakespeare and Einstein, pacemakers in the sciences and arts, who have given us a greater appreciation of truth and beauty, so we shall evolve social pacemakers —men who will teach us fundamental truths about life in community. I believe that Gandhi and Bertrand Russell are two such men. We have moved on from the Survival of the Fittest to the Survival of the Highest—and what an exciting era this is both to observe and participate in!

So I glory in the fact that Man shares a common heritage

with the animal world. It is through the struggle against his animal instincts that his conscience develops and he slowly humanises himself.

*   *   *

What about those qualities which are unique in Man? I would give priority to his capacity for suffering. As an exponent of the philosophy of non-violence, I have given much thought to the role and function of suffering in human life and I am convinced that Man alone of all life has the capacity to suffer as opposed to merely feeling pain. Suffering is the ability to understand and use pain in a constructive way. Did not Jesus Christ, the very pattern of Man, use suffering, and only suffering to accomplish his work? Pain brings out the very highest or the very lowest in Man—it will either degrade him and reduce him to the animal, or it can be used creatively to accomplish some purpose. Strike a dog and it will feel pain, and that is all; strike a child and he will suffer, not because he feels an unpleasant sensation but because he senses a change in relationship. The key to the philosophy of non-violence is that it transforms pain into suffering. It welcomes the pain inflicted by others and uses it to alter relationships.

The very attempts of modern societies to insulate themselves from suffering have resulted in a refusal of love, for the willingness to love and be loved makes suffering inevitable. And in the refusal of love, modern man feels pain without the possibility of transforming it into suffering. In trying to shut out suffering, Man only turns it into something useless and degrading. To be a Man implies a willingness to accept the responsibility and dignity of suffering; where this capacity is lost, Man once again takes his place in the animal world.

Man too has a name. I am not thinking of the label given to the whole species but to the means by which we are identified and distinguished from each other. The people of Africa are rich in names. It is the product of their humanism. To be known by name is to be dependent, linked with the one who utters it, and to know all a man's names is to have a special claim upon him. In Africa, our names are of many sorts. There is our tribal or clan name. Then there is often a special name which describes some experience or desirable attributes or records some significant event. My own middle name is Buchizya—the Unexpected One—because I was born long after natural expectancy had died in my parents. Often, there is added to this string of names the so-called Christian name, which was originally given to baptised Christians by missionaries to show that they had broken with their old life and now belonged to Christ. Very often the use of this Christian name degenerated into a matter of mere convenience. It was less trouble to the White Man to dub a servant John or David than to go to the trouble of learning his true name, which would be to demean himself and come down to the African's level.

I could go on for a long time on the significance of names in our culture. The importance of Man having a name is that it speaks both of his uniqueness and of his dependence upon others. Because he is called by name there is no one else on earth quite like him. This is, of course, literally true because no other individual can share the same point in space and time. Every man is unrepeatable; once and for all. Yet he is a dependent being—a member of a family, a work situation and a community. And because he has a name it is possible to enter into relationship with him. Is it not the tension between that element in his nature in which he differs from all others and the element which he shares with them that produces most of the great things of which he is capable?

Man was intended to be an end in himself; this is surely implied by the Bible's claim that he is 'made in the image of God' and has been given 'dominion over all living things'.

But he has been reduced to a means. The industrialist uses him as a means to wealth. To the demagogue he is the means to power, to the selfish lover the means of gratification. The war-monger uses him as cannon-fodder; to the economist he is a statistic; to the mass entertainer, he is an instrument to be manipulated. Everywhere Man is being used. And once he becomes a means to an end then all his abilities and activities can be exploited and organised to serve the interests of the nation, the State or the society. He ceases to be the absolute standard by which all systems should be measured. Instead he has to twist his personality and reduce his stature in order to fit into the system. I feel that there is a paradox here. The social and political units of the modern world are at one and the same time so large that Man is lost within them, yet so small that he cannot realise his potentiality. In the modern mass institution, he is physically too small to count, yet morally and intellectually he dwarfs it.

A politician like myself must always be alive to this danger of using man as a means rather than an end. We can so easily subordinate him to the interests of national pride, international prestige or what is called efficient government. And we can only avoid doing this by having faith in him and creating the conditions of life which will enable him to justify this faith.

No doubt the critics will claim that I expect too much of Man and the theologians will take issue with me for not giving due weight to Original Sin or the evil inherent in personal and social life which seems so often to have frustrated all Man's hopes and dreams. Their comments are, no doubt, justified. I can only retort that there are enough critics *against* Man. I am *for* him! Theologians, political scientists, sociologists and psychologists have had a good innings denigrating Man. It is time his defenders entered the lists. Possibly I do not take this volume of criticism as seriously as I ought because as far as I am concerned Man is not an abstraction, the subject of a theological sermon or a philosophical thesis. Man means my mother, my wife, my children, my friends, the citizens of my country. They deserve my faith. They shall have it.

3

African Adjustment to Independence

I have been giving some thought to the effect which Independence has upon the people of former Colonial territories. In terms of the speed of change and the radical alteration in the structure of social and political institutions, it would not be out of place to describe the situation as revolutionary. Very little, if any, blood has been spilt and everything is done in a constitutional manner, yet the psychic shock to the people must be very similar to that they would feel if there had been a violent overthrow of one government and its replacement by another operating on a different basis. Certainly, the more enlightened colonial powers do phase the change-over in such a way that officials and nationalist leaders can prepare the minds of the people to a certain extent. But I am sure that not enough thought has been given to what might loosely be termed the psychological problems created by the attempts of African and non-African citizens to adjust themselves to a radical change in the power-structure of the newly independent State. The political, economic and constitutional problems which Independence brings in its wake have been exhaustively treated; psychological problems tend to be ignored, possibly because nationalists do not wish to give aid and comfort to their enemies who claim that the peoples of Africa are not 'ready' for Independence. Yet it is only common sense to recognise that adjustment to change is

48

something which all human beings find difficult, whether in Africa or elsewhere in the world. I am too involved in the day-to-day problems of Zambia to have the leisure to study this subject in depth. Nor have I the specialist training in psychology which would be necessary. But this is an urgent problem and important area for research to which our universities and research institutions should be giving priority. In the meantime, here are some thoughts on the problem of adjustment which, though they lack the objectivity of the detached observer, at least have the authority of personal experience. I myself am currently engaged in making this process of adjustment to the demands of a new society and I am in a strategic position from which to observe my fellow citizens doing the same.

A realistic starting point for discussion is a statement of fact, at once blindingly obvious and yet prone to be ignored by some of our citizens. It takes more than the lowering of a Union Jack, the stroke of a pen and the passing of an act of Parliament to wipe out the past. However exciting the vistas that open up before a newly independent State; however radically different the power-structure of the new state from the old; it is still the same *old* people who constitute the *new* state. No blessed amnesia steals over them on the morning after Independence Day. They carry with them into the new society as part of their baggage the experience and heritage of their colonial past in spite of all their attempts to wipe the slate clean. Human nature is not, in the short run, changed by constitutional instruments.

Human beings are not as malleable as constitutions. People are to a great extent what the past has made them, and therefore there are severe limitations upon the speed and effectiveness with which they can adjust to a new society. Any government which ignores this elementary truth will both suffer grave disillusionment and add appreciably to the mountain of problems inherited from its predecessors. A wise government, whilst recognising that the people want quick results, will also take account of the psychological effects of radical change, and therefore, go to great lengths to ensure that the underlying logic of their policies is understood and that the people are moving with them.

The sledge-hammer impact of colonialism and its camp-follower industrialisation has done much to mould the shape of the African peoples' past. Even when the formal symbols of colonialism have been removed its ghost-like presence persists, psychologically conditioning a people who stand politically and constitutionally independent. This of course is not a permanent state of affairs and it is one we are determined to change as quickly as possible, but it is a factor to be taken into account during the perilous early years of independence.

What is the psychological legacy left by colonialism? I see it as a series of contradictions—a strange mixture of advantages and disadvantages, curses and blessings.

Colonialism brought greater freedom yet more servitude. The peoples of Africa were freed from certain enemies—disease, ignorance, superstition and slavery—the horizons of their lives were lifted, offering new areas of choice and fresh possibilities of material and spiritual enrichment.

Yet the colonialism which threw open certain doors, slammed others shut. It engendered in the African peoples a deepening awareness of servitude. New forms of power cast a web about them, hemming them in and subjecting them to strange constraints. As the Century of Democracy wore on, an awareness that they were ruled well no longer compensated them for not ruling themselves. Because Europeans had a monopoly of power and skills, it was inevitable that they should assume positions of leadership and control, the original tribal societies being unable to withstand the impact of their aggressive presence. But all too often this practical superiority was transformed into a philosophy of racial dominance. It appeared that the colonialists had freed them in order to make them servants.

Colonialism brought us greater security yet more precariousness. Colonial rule resulted in the application of a uniform system of law which, backed by superior force and generally equably administered, gave the African peoples a new sense of security. They were no longer at the mercy of arbitrary forms of power. In the economic field, those who became part of the money economy were freed from the vagaries of Nature, being less susceptible to famine, drought and blight.

But a new precariousness too characterised their lives. With all its limitations, the tribal structure offered its members an identity, an assured place, and a network of ritual solutions to life's problems. Industrial society on the other hand confronted them with situations to which these ritual solutions were no longer relevant. They became, to paraphrase A. E. Housman, 'strangers and afraid, in a world they never made . . .'.

Colonialism brought us greater fellowship yet more loneliness. Men who had regarded the inhabitants of the next village as strangers began to move freely around the country, striking up new relationships based upon individual choice rather than tribal solidarity. New associations developed—political parties, trade unions, social clubs, churches. As political consciousness grew, they became aware of their 'Africanness', sharing a common ideology with groups from which they had been traditionally isolated.

But urbanisation, which brought men together, also effectively separated them out into lone units, having to fend for themselves and feeling infinitely remote from the village's little welfare state where the old, the sick and the incapable were accepted as legitimate charges upon the charity of all. The unquestioning support of the extended family and clan were not so easily laid hold upon, and men knew rootlessness until nationalism swept them up and gave them a new affinity to replace lost kinships.

Colonialism brought greater attainment yet more failure.

Industrialisation provides great opportunities for the realisation of human potential. Economic competitiveness is a philosophy which sets its own standards of attainment and richly rewards those who can match them. Social mobility becomes possible, enabling men to be judged not by what they were born but by what they can make of themselves by effort of will and muscle and brain.

Yet the opportunity of attainment implies the possibility of failure. It is easy to romanticise the tribal way of life as a vestige of some Golden Age, but as I have written elsewhere, the tribe did not take account of failure. No one need feel discarded because he could not make the grade, whereas those who failed to reach the rigorous standards of administrative and economic efficiency demanded by industrial society felt useless and unwanted.

It would be churlish to blind oneself to the positive contribution of the colonial powers to the development of Africa. But honesty compels us to recognise that the colonial impact has sown confusion and set up tensions in the minds of the African people which add appreciably to the difficulties facing the governments of independent African states. The ideology of nationalism has undone much of the harm caused by the ambiguities of colonialism; it has restored our people's self-respect and given them a sense of identification with the new nation. But at the point of Independence, we were a people under tension, and a tension not of our own making—a factor to be borne in mind by the captious critics who perch on our shoulders crying doom upon our great adventure in nation-building.

*   *   *

It is a lesson of history and experience that nothing succeeds in uniting people so effectively as the struggle against a common enemy. Traditional differences are forgotten, internecine strife ceases and all the energy of the people is harnessed to drive them towards one goal. In Africa, colonialism has provided a convenient if hardly warlike Common Enemy in opposition to which a people, traditionally divided along tribal, linguistic and regional lines, achieves unity. In its militant phase, nationalism is the great solvent of traditional divisions. Intellectuals stand shoulder to shoulder with peasants, urban dwellers with rural folk, and personal enmities between leaders of the people are played down in order that all eyes may be focused upon the one target—the dispossession of the colonial power.

Nationalism is made up of a whole complex of factors and it is certainly not my intention to imply that its strength or effectiveness depends upon the existence of a Common Enemy. Nevertheless, in political terms, the presence of the Common Enemy greatly accelerates the growth of nationalist feeling. To the ordinary man in the street, ideologies and political theories do not mean much. It is difficult to rouse his interest or get him to identify himself with a theoretical political programme. But the Common Enemy affects his life in some way or another whether he be an intellectual, a peasant, an industrial worker or a farmer. Hence the nationalist leader can dramatise the freedom struggle more effectively by declaring war upon the Common Enemy than by cold political analyses and argument.

Once the Common Enemy is removed, the citizens of an independent state find themselves on their own in a cold, hard world where clear judgement of their calibre is not obscured by the presence, inhibiting or otherwise, of an alien factor. The leaders of modern Africa ask no quarter in the world's judgement of their performance. They expect to be assessed by the highest standards of efficiency and responsibility without the ambiguities of colonialism blurring the picture. It must be admitted however, that certain elements in their societies, having been weighed in the balance of achievement and found wanting, may cast around for other scapegoats to replace colonialism and in so doing revive traditional tribal or regional animosities. For a tiny, disgruntled minority, colonialism has been a built-in scapegoat, on to which could be projected responsibility for lack of attainment. With the removal of the Common Enemy, there is no longer a *they* to take the blame for *our* failures. We must stand or fall without the aid of the colonial crutch. This is the supreme test of the character of our people. Most welcome the opportunity of showing what they can do. A few, who would be failures with or without the colonial presence, find themselves exposed in their inadequacy.

Inevitably, the overthrow of the Common Enemy takes some of the dynamism out of nationalism, or rather it moves it into a phase where its aims cannot be so simply and dramatically depicted. This falling-off of momentum is a particular challenge to the party, whose function is crucial in the early days of independence, since it may be the only surviving structure of communication and control between Government and the mass of the people until such time as the replacement of colonial administrative institutions is carried through. But the party will be undergoing its own crisis, its able officials creamed off to fill diplomatic and administrative posts and good replacements hard to attract to jobs where the zest and excitement of the independence struggle gives place to office routine. Thus Dr Julius Nyerere, when Prime Minister of Tanganyika, regarded this particular problem as sufficiently acute to resign his office in order to direct personally the reorganisation of the national party. I want us to look at the whole question of the future of nationalism, so I will not develop this point at the present time.

The vacuum left, psychologically speaking, by the departure of the Common Enemy must be filled. The ideology of nationalism must find a new mode of expression which will stir the people to throw themselves wholeheartedly into the work of nation-building. We African leaders are well aware of the potency of the Common Enemy concept and want to give it a new twist by calling our people to make war upon the elemental problems such as hunger and unemployment which threaten the existence of our State. These are the new, impersonal Common Enemy. 'Freedom!' as a watchword must be given an essential qualification—'Freedom through Hard Work!' The stirring calls once made for the people to stand shoulder to shoulder against the colonialist must now go out as an appeal to tackle together great social and economic problems. It is however a lamentable fact about human nature that it is not so easy to heat the blood by enunciating a positive ideology as it is through such negative but evocative slogans as 'The Colonialist Must Go!' It is not so easy to get the people to sit down to a banquet of unemployment statistics as it is to have them feed upon their grievances. But it must be done! By personal example, the power of the party and skilful use of propaganda, the people must be made to realise that these new impersonal Common Enemies are as great a threat to their nationhood as ever the colonialist were.

Less responsible national leaders may try to take the easy way out and attempt to buy national unity by building up neighbouring nations as a new Commony Enemy, or by a witch hunt for real or fancied subversive elements within their own borders. Abstractions such as Neo-Colonialism and Communism may become propaganda targets in order to divert the minds of the people from Government's failure to meet their expectations. I am not saying that such outside Common Enemies do not exist. The white-dominated nations at the southern tip of the Continent are a threat to Africa's peace and security. What I am saying is that it is immoral, and in the long run futile, to delude the people by trying to divert the strong emotion which would otherwise be directed against oneself onto an outside Common Enemy. The leader of a nation has a representative responsibility. He must expect to be held to account if things go wrong and ought not to complain of injustice or victimisation. It is the abnegation of leadership to attempt to 'get out from under' when responsibility has to be assigned.

Time is the scarcest of all Africa's resources. The preoccupation of the leaders of the new Africa is to purchase enough of it in which to establish a record of positive achievement which will give the people hope. To change the metaphor, they have got to get the roof on before the foundations crack—a task made more formidable by the anticlimactic atmosphere which is the inevitable aftermath of Independence.

*   *   *

I want to draw attention to another factor which makes adjustment to Independence difficult. This is the psychological restiveness of the people due to the persistence of political frustration built up during the years of the independence struggle. Indeed, British colonial policy might be said to have encouraged the growth of such political frustration through its emphasis upon constitutional advance against increasing pressure—widespread evidence of the people's frustration being taken as a signal for further concessions.

But political frustration built up over years cannot be dissipated overnight. It takes more than exuberant participation in Independence celebrations to work it off. It persists beyond the removal of its rational causes. It is highly significant for example, that the Copperbelt of what was then Northern Rhodesia saw the greatest degree of violence and political disturbance, not during the height of the independence struggle when the future was uncertain, but in 1963 when the issue was beyond doubt. The end of colonial rule was clearly in sight, the promise to dismantle the Federation had been given, there was an African majority in the Legislature and a coalition nationalist Government in power, yet in spite of all these earnests of the future, political frustration reached crisis point.

The psychologist defines frustration as the condition which occurs when a blockage is placed in the way of some desired goal resulting in the destructive outworking of the energy generated to achieve it. He further claims that the symptoms of frustration are aggression, heightened suggestibility and a reversion to non-constructive patterns of behaviour. All these conditions are likely to be experienced in the immediate post-independence period, and only the passage of time, and the displacement of the people's pent-up energy into constructive channels will allay them. In the meantime, nationalist leaders have got to find some means of disarming this psychological time-bomb in the minds of the people before it explodes.

*   *   *

The *négritude* debate has drawn attention to the fact that the question being asked all over Black Africa is 'Who am I?' —it is the search for a stratum of experience which is neither a colonial importation nor a legacy of the tribal past; it is the attempt to discover what it means to be a *modern* African. I cannot help feeling that to a certain extent this *négritude* cult is an intellectual exercise, drawing distinctions which may seem clear-cut in the university lecture room and school of African studies, but nothing like so consciously felt by the people on the ground in Africa. I do admit that Western influence has been so pervasive that it is not easy to point to elements in contemporary African society, other than the purely traditional, which have not been touched and changed by it. Certainly a proud, politically independent people desire to create a society whose ethos and institutions reflect their essential genius. As a result, a tension may be set up between the desire to do things in a boldly different way from the colonialist, and the reasonable fear that the consequences of daring innovation may be disastrous.

Yet there must be continuity between the past and the

future, especially in those States committed to operating the sophisticated economic and bureaucratic institutions the colonialists have left behind them. As I have said elsewhere, there is no valid choice between an African and European method of balancing a budget or of administering and controlling large governmental and public agencies. There are only right ways and wrong ways. Since the colonialist was not always wrong, his nationalist successor may find himself perpetuating a system he once pledged himself to overthrow. The mass of the people, being unaware of the subtleties of economics, know only that *our* society looks just like *their* society did. Only the more sophisticated can see a valid distinction between decisions taken by a fully representative government and those, apparently identical, taken by the colonialist. The trend toward African socialism is, of course, an attempt to resolve this dilemma by evolving an economic system consonant with the genius of the African people.

Historically, the peoples of Africa had no social identity larger than the tribe, except for certain great nations, most of which no longer exist. We have the colonialists to thank (or blame!) for drawing national boundaries and establishing overall administration and communication. But it takes more than a continuous line on the map to give people a sense of national identity. This search for national identity underlies all the detailed problems which the independent State faces. The people will perch indecisively between alternative patterns of behaviour until there is a genuine consensus on what is the Zambian, Tanzanian or Kenyan way of doing things.

Nowhere is the lack of a clear-cut behaviour pattern more obviously revealed than in the attitudes of African citizens to European members of their society in the immediate post-independence period. Racial attitudes hardened over generations are not easily reversed. Some Africans find it difficult to come to terms with the fact that the Gods are dead, or at least that stripped of their divinity, they walk the earth like other men! Some Europeans, whilst outwardly conforming to the demands of the new situation, still demonstrate racial arrogance by a look in the eye and a tone in the voice. Thus, there is a wide range of mutual response between the two races. Suspicion and misunderstanding may poison the atmosphere as the people of both races struggle to encounter each other as fellow human beings in defiance of the conditioning of the past. Much of the people's psychic energy is dissipated until they learn to follow acceptable patterns of behaviour—the Zambian way of doing things.

It is primarily through the evolution of a genuine culture that a people discover their national identity. But cultural growth may be inhibited by the reluctance of a government in straightened financial circumstances to devote some of its resources to the encouragement of activities—sculpture, visual arts, writing, music and drama—which many of the people would regard as irrelevant to national development. Universities, too, tend to be strictly utilitarian in scope, turning out a stream of the technical, professional and scientific people required in the central areas of nation-building, and having neither the resources nor the personnel to devote to such rarefied subjects as fine arts and theology. Yet the nation which lacks a firm cultural substructure is jerry-built and though the people have title deeds to the property and the key to the front door in their pockets, they are still homeless.

To describe post-independence problems of adjustment in this way is not to imply any pessimism about the future of the new states of Africa. It would be equally foolish either to ignore the existence of such problems or to behave as though they were insuperable. You once used a phrase—Optimism of Grace—which I like very much. There is such an 'optimism of grace' at work in the new Africa which scorns the predictions of doom which are heaped upon her.

Let me quote in return some words of Aimé Césaire, which express the spirit of African nationalism:

For it is not true at all that the work of man is finished,
that we have nothing more to do in the world,
that it is enough that we should set ourselves in the steps of the
    world,
but the work of man is only beginning,
and it remains for man to conquer every immobilised prohibition
    at the corners of his zeal,
and no race possesses the monopoly of beauty, intelligence, force,
and there is room for all of us at the rendezvous of victory.

4

Non-African Adjustment to Independence

I was interested in your comments on the problems facing our European citizens in adjusting to Independence. Obviously, you should know more about this subject than I since you are yourself undergoing this process of adjustment. This is how the problem strikes me.

If you were to feed the truth drug to our European citizens I have little doubt that many of them would confess that at the point of Independence they felt that the take-over was premature; that the British Government ought to have resisted African political pressures in order to win a longer period of transition. This was the rationale behind European support for the Federation of Rhodesia and Nyasaland. Though they knew perfectly well that Northern Rhodesia (as it then was) was being penalised because the whole system had a built-in bias towards Southern Rhodesia, they were prepared to back the Federation to the very end because they saw it as a brake upon African advancement in the North. They thought that Sir Roy Welensky was big enough and tough enough to withstand both internal and external pressures towards constitutional change and that he and his Government would decide on what terms and at what speed Africans would be allowed political, economic and social advancement.

Europeans who felt this way were blinding themselves

to the signs writ large in the skies over post-war Africa. They were shouting against the wind. It was inevitable that Northern Rhodesia should go the same way as the territories to the North of her. Indeed, Europeans should be grateful to the British Government for not attempting to hold off Independence any longer for there is no doubt that the patience of the African people was exhausted. I know this better than anyone because as President of UNIP I had to withstand mounting demands within the Party and from the people as a whole for a stepping-up of Cha-Cha-Cha—sabotage and civil disobedience. Had we reached the point of an armed showdown, when the dust had settled there would have been no place for Europeans here.

However, good sense prevailed and my people were granted self-rule in the nick of time. But that stormy pre-independence period has left its scars. Many Europeans, feeling bitterly resentful at what they regarded as a 'sell-out' by the British Government, approached Independence in a negative frame of mind, fearful of the future. Possibly they were afraid that we Africans might return the compliment and treat them to a dose of the same 'partnership' they had offered us!

The undoubted success of our first year of independence, characterised by racial harmony and an increasing sense of national purpose, has, I know, reassured many of our European population, who have been magnanimous enough to confess that their lack of confidence in us was ill-founded. But others have adopted as their motto that lame saying of Asquith 'Let's wait and see . . .' They sit with their bags mentally packed, anxiously scanning the horizon for the first sign of an impending storm.

Now as I see it, there can be no adjustment to a new society without *commitment*—a willingness to identify oneself with a country's destiny, rejoicing in its hopes, sharing its fears, standing firm in times of hardship. Our African people have forged ahead with the process of adjustment because they are utterly committed to this great experiment in Human Relations. They are here for eternity, with no hiding place, no bolt-hole anywhere else in Africa or the world. If Zambia should collapse then they will go down with her. Unlike some Europeans, they do not live in a constant state of mental indecision, trying to balance the advantages of life here in Zambia against those somewhere else.

Modern Africa is no place for the uncommitted. Life here demands cool nerves, perpetual optimism and great faith in human possibilities. Those who live with their bags mentally packed are of all men the most miserable. They are like hypochondriacs, taking their temperature and feeling their pulse every hour to see whether they are still fit. They are blind to the positive aspects of Independence. They do not notice the immense verve and dedication of our people—their gritted-teeth determination to make Zambia great—because they are utterly preoccupied with the search for cracks in the foundation. They magnify every isolated incident into a full-blown calamity. Every loose stone heralds an avalanche, every gust of wind a tornado. They wish to feast upon the fruits of our prosperity but will slink off at the first sign of adversity.

This kind of approach can spell only unhappiness and insecurity. To demand brass-bound guarantees that one will be preserved from challenge and difficulty as a condition for residence in an African State is to demand the impossible. Africa is a continent in ferment at the heart of an unstable world. There is no spot on the Globe devoid of difficulty and even danger in these times. In the United States, there is increasing military commitment in Viet Nam; in Asia, famine; in South Africa, growing isolation and racial tension; in Britain, economic difficulty and radical readjustment. Identify yourself with any of these nations and you are committed for better or worse, in prosperity or adversity. If the nation is wounded, you must bleed with it, just as you are entitled to feel pride in its achievements.

I suspect that some Europeans were drawn to colonial Africa as a kind of Cloud-Cuckoo-Land, where they could live a fairy-tale existence, comfortably insulated from hard reality. Now because the dream has been shattered, they are looking around anxiously for some alternative Garden of Eden. They are unlikely to find one.

This is a time for plain speaking. The truth is that except in the most obvious sense, many of our European residents have not been conscious of living in Africa at all. They exported to the African continent a segment of Europe, within which, sheltered by a sympathetic Colonial Government which often placed their welfare above that of the indigenous peoples, they could enjoy a privileged existence which might be described as better-class suburbia without the fog and cold. The other Africa, with its poverty, disease, ignorance and unemployment, never really impinged upon their consciousness. If it did, they shrugged it off as a responsibility of the Colonial Power. Now this other Africa occupies the foreground; it cannot be hidden or ignored. It is the main preoccupation of the Governments of independent States. They fought for freedom in order to banish these centuries-old scourges of their peoples for ever. These giant spectres did not emerge at the point of Independence as some Europeans fondly imagine. They have been there all along, but now all the blinkers are off—Europeans together with all other citizens of the nation must look them in the face and also accept a share of responsibility in helping to overcome them.

Yet are there not great compensations in living at a time and in a place where any man or woman of mettle and character can decisively affect the course of events by his sincere efforts? In the advanced, mammoth nations of the West, the contribution of the individual, however useful, seems to have little effect. Here in Africa, the dedicated man or woman can see the results of his work dramatically depicted before his eyes. Some stone in the edifice of the nation is his very own, a permanent testimony to his contribution. And the efforts of that individual are correspondingly valued by the people who receive his service. One teacher, doctor, engineer or farmer in Zambia, makes a difference. We have not got endless reserves of human resource. It is a cliché of the West that no man is indispensable. Maybe so; but in the new states of Africa it is more likely that what a talented and dedicated individual refuses or is unable to do will remain undone—an unfilled gap in the walls which must weaken the whole structure. I should have thought, therefore, that nations like Zambia offer to Europeans the opportunity for exercising those gifts of mind and heart and muscle which helped once to make the Western nations great.

*   *   *

I certainly take your point that Zambia is not, in the accepted sense of the word, settler country, and that the majority of non-Zambians are here for a limited period of their lives, determined beforehand and unrelated to recent political developments. Possibly they said to themselves that they would live and work in Africa until their children were a certain age, or until they had accumulated a given amount of capital which would allow them to realise long-sought ambitions—to buy a farm or a small business and so on. You put it well, I think, when you say that Zambia provides the opportunity for foreign workers, through the investment of a certain slice of their lives, to become capitalists. Good luck to them, providing their wealth is not earned by the exploitation of our people.

The lawyers tell me that the legal definition of one's domicile is that it is the place where one hopes to die. I am well aware that for only a small minority of Europeans will this country be their domicile. And as far as I and my people are concerned, there are no hard feelings about this.

Expatriates who have done an honest day's work have made a contribution to Zambia's welfare for which our people are grateful. When such folk leave, they may go in peace with our thanks and blessing, and I trust they will enjoy the benefits of their work.

Of such transient residents of our country we ask only one thing. They must recognise that they are the guests of our people. The days have gone when they could impose their way of life and pattern of society upon us. They are in many ways spectators in this struggle to build a nation, and must recognise that there are limits to the amount of noise they can make on the touch-line. For this game in which our Government is engaged involves the destiny of four million people and we cannot afford to be distracted. We therefore expect such spectators to avoid getting under our feet and hindering our progress. This is not an unreasonable thing to demand. After all, there is nothing to stop them coming onto the field with us, provided they are prepared to see the game out to its end, win or lose.

*   *   *

The biggest hindrance to Europeans becoming psychologically adjusted to Independence is the fact that for so long they have been accustomed to a society organised for their benefit and convenience, that any change must be for the worse. And since changes are occurring now thick and fast, they tend to regard such changes as directed against them, as though a malevolent Government in Lusaka spent much of its time thinking up policies aimed at intimidating or victimising them. In fact, the changes which are occuring daily are directed *against* no one. They are the structural changes necessary in order to create a more just and equitable society. This must mean the greater sharing of wealth, the end of exclusiveness and racial privilege, and the offer of opportunities to those who have been denied all the elements of the good life—education, health, responsibility and a fair return for labour. Possibly, some of these changes may work, on the short term, to the disadvantage of our European communities, but if they are honest, they should admit that they will only be losing what they ought never to have had —those privileges unrelated to ability and contribution; false valuations arrived at by racial consideration.

To give a specific example. It has been suggested that our Zambianisation policy in Government and industry, etc., is a denial of our avowed constitutional aim of creating a non-racial society in which men will be judged and rewarded as individuals, race and colour apart. What these critics forget, of course, is that there is no chance of even beginning to build a non-racial society on the historical foundations we inherited from the colonialists . . . for how can a Zambian, denied education, advancement and positions of responsibility compete on equal terms with expatriates who have had the benefit of all these things over a long period of time? Therefore, our present Zambianisation policy is not the extreme swing of the pendulum from the end of the arc labelled *European* to that labelled *Zambian*, but the attempt to get the pendulum back to a central position before setting it in motion again. We have first to clean up a historically accumulated mess and give Zambians the fair opportunities of advancement they have been so long denied, before we can move on to that stage of friendly competitiveness between Zambians and non-Zambians in the economic and administrative sectors of our society—the 'best man for the job' concept—which is what we understand by a non-racial policy.

It is the ultimate of unrealism for Europeans to imagine that a nation can win its independence without changes occurring which decisively affect their lives. We do not expect them necessarily to *like* such changes, but we do expect them to recognise that these changes do not result from our desire to penalise Europeans, but are the outworkings of our avowed intention to create a just society.

For over half a century, the indigenous peoples of Africa have been exposed to the psychology of the European—they have been until recently the passive recipients of whatever treatment Europeans cared to dole out to them. The advent of independence spells the end of a European-orientated society—Europeans will be increasingly exposed to African psychology. They are now part of a society in which the initiatives are no longer exclusively theirs, and where, in many fields, they will cease to be *doers* and become *acceptors*. This is a hard fact of life and Africa is no place for any European who cannot accept it. To come to terms with this truth is the essential condition of a happy, well-adjusted life in Zambia.

*   *   *

You ask me to spell out in more detail my statement that Europeans need to become accustomed to being *acceptors* rather than *doers* in the new Zambia. My point is this. There is an aggressive self-confidence about the Western mind, to whose questings so many of the problems and mysteries of the world have succumbed. Europeans, therefore, find it difficult to imagine a better way of doing things than their own. They observe the difference between the methods and aims of our present Government and those of its colonial predecessor and conclude that where they deviate they must be inferior. Now this might be true if our aim and intention in Zambia were to create a 'black' version of colonial society. It is not. The underlying motive of all our methods and policies is the creation of a modern African society—a society which will reflect the genius of our people. Hence many of our ways of going about things will appear strange to Europeans, but that is not to say that we are wrong or that we do not know what we are doing. They will find it impossible to judge realistically the effectiveness of our policies unless they also understand our goal, and this in turn calls for a greater degree of identification with our society than many of them are prepared to make.

So acceptance, then, is the price of European adjustment to our new society—acceptance of that fact that they are now part of an African society, some facets of which are bound to be strange and puzzling to them. And if they would have peace of mind, they must resist the temptation to jump to the conclusion that every deviation from the colonial system is evidence of a deterioration which will eventually lead to chaos. Our methods are different but it has yet to be proved that in the long run they are less effective.

It is always a hazardous business to change the very foundations of a society, and it can never be done without a certain degree of social and economic dislocation. I and my colleagues are responsibly aware of the dangers inherent in the course of action to which we are committed, but the inequities and irrelevancies of the colonial structure we inherited leave us no alternative. Our duty to our people impels us to press ahead with the creation of a modern African State as swiftly as possible. Europeans, witnessing this gigantic operation, may understandably find the spectacle somewhat nerve-racking. But they might reflect upon the truth that had more been done during the period they had a monopoly of political power to create representative institutions of government and spread more widely economic and social justice, the changes they are now undergoing would have been less radical.

*   *   *

My last point leads me to the following observation. No group can ever view with equanimity the loss of political power. This truth exposes the fallacy of the 'gradualist' solution to the problems of Rhodesia and South Africa—this glorious myth that the White minorities who enjoy a monopoly of political power will voluntarily relinquish it in stages in favour of the unenfranchised majorities in their countries as they judge them to be 'ready' to exercise it.

It would be a miracle indeed for minorities, nurtured for generations upon racist thinking, to commit themselves willingly into the hands of black majorities whom they have been taught are still a thousand years away from so-called civilisation. Had the Federation of Rhodesia and Nyasaland been granted independence under Sir Roy Welensky and his Government, can anyone seriously claim that Zambia and Malawi would now be enjoying self-rule? And given the intensity of African feeling shortly before the break-up of the Federation, it is clear that a full-scale racial war would now be raging here. It took the *force majeure* of Britain to impose upon unwilling Whites a solution which, apparently against their interests, has nevertheless resulted in a society, virtually free of racial tension, in which they can still enjoy a good life.

Now the purpose of this apparent digression is to underline the point that I am well aware of the apprehension Europeans or anyone else must feel when they lose their grip upon the reigns of political power. After all, I and my people know what it is like to be politically powerless. But what I want to make clear is that we have not won a monopoly of political power in order to use it in some tit-for-tat way to bring retribution upon the heads of Europeans. There are obviously many Europeans who, whilst admitting that so far Africans have not used their political supremacy in order to avenge themselves for past insults and injustices, are convinced that the present harmonious relations are just the lull before a storm of retribution about to break over their heads. Now this apprehension must be the fruit of their uneasy consciences rather than the result of any policy we have pursued since independence. I say again, the African people are a forgiving people. In any case, we cannot spare the time to pay off old scores. There is urgent work to be done. So paradoxically, the loss of political power by

Europeans in Zambia has made it possible for them to become a valued part of a new society, whereas the attempt to cling on to it would have made them the centre of a racial holocaust too terrible to contemplate.

*   *   *

Whilst I am happy to offer any reasonable reassurance to all Europeans of goodwill, there is a small minority who merit only a stern warning. They have become prophets of doom, confidently predicting that an independent Zambia will collapse in bankruptcy and chaos, and they are emotionally committed to their predictions. Their reputations as prophets of doom are at stake amongst their fellow-Europeans. Hence, they magnify every slight difficulty or isolated incident in order to help make their prognostications come true. They are spreaders of rumour and disaffection. They *want* to see Zambia fail, provided of course that they have safely retired to their bolt-holes in South Africa, Britain or elsewhere.

Now for all our forgiveness and tolerance as a people, one thing we do demand of everyone, white and black, is loyalty to Zambia. And loyalty is beyond no one's power to give. Those Whites who are not prepared to offer it will find Zambia a hard and inhospitable place. We shall have no more mercy upon them than any nation at war would have upon traitors in its midst. I repeat, the price of our tolerance is loyalty to the State.

I do not belittle the difficulties that Europeans face in adjusting themselves to our new society. They cannot be expected to make this adjustment painlessly or without effort, and this my Government understands. But if they are to feel at home amongst us, they must try sincerely to rise to the challenge of radical change. They feel cold and unloved because they stand shivering on the edge of the pool, unable to make up their minds whether to jump in or retreat to more congenial surroundings. If only they would take the plunge, they might find the water much warmer than they imagine.

*   *   *

I have never made the mistake of under-valuing the European contribution to Zambia through administrators, missionaries, professional men, farmers and industrial workers. Because the institutions of government were, on the whole, in good shape when they were handed over to us, and partly because of European technical and economic competence, we were able to take-off into independence from a lofty platform. But Europeans must realise that they cannot live indefinitely upon their inherited capital of good-will. We are not so much interested in being told what they have done *for* us in the past as in learning what they are prepared to do *alongside* us in the future. To work as a col-league alongside someone who before was the recipient of one's patronage calls for a quality of humility that Europeans have not had much opportunity to develop during their stay in Africa. But I have always understood that European civilisation blossomed because a whole people were capable of rising to the challenge of change, of grasping quickly new opportunities and of abandoning old and outmoded ways of thought and action. For Europeans in Africa, there is now the challenge of adjusting to change *which they themselves have not initiated*, for which they can claim little credit and whose direction they cannot control. The ability of Europeans to do this will be the acid test of their survival in Africa.

*   *   *

Now I have some words of advice to offer those Europeans who wish to identify themselves with our new society and have a sense of commitment to it. We are grateful for their colleagueship and welcome them to our ranks. In general, the struggle for adjustment of such kindred spirits of ours will be much easier because, in most cases, these Europeans have made the encounter of their African fellow-citizens as friends and colleagues before the advent of independence.

It is truly tragic the fear which has been engendered in European minds because they now find themselves ruled by black strangers, fellow-citizens of whom they have no understanding whatever because in the years prior to independence these Europeans made no attempt to get to know their black neighbours as *people*. They met Africans only on their own terms, within the context of a fixed and limited relationship. They would claim that, from long experience, they *knew* the African. Possibly they did know the African as servant and employee—as an extension of a broom or a shovel, but too few Europeans took the trouble to get to know him as a fellow human being. Certainly, they showed kindness and even generosity to those Africans they encountered in business relationships. They gave them many things—coddled them when ill; helped to educate their children; treated them with a certain fond indulgence. They gave many things. But they did not give themselves. These relationships tended to be one-way, with the European dictating the degree of intimacy, deciding what he would give to and what he would withhold from the relationship. There was lacking that basic honesty and openness of true friendship. Possibly there were faults on both sides, but the consequence of that period of artificiality in relations between the races is that many Europeans may as well be ruled by men from Mars in terms of the understanding they now have of their African fellow citizens. On the other hand, those Europeans who did establish genuine links across the racial barrier are free from fear because they know that they are amongst friends. They have some degree of insight into the African mind and so can avoid the misunderstandings which worry many of their European neighbours.

Now a point or two for these sympathetic Europeans.

In the first place, they should avoid trying to become white Africans. You will remember that in the days of the Federation certain Africans, seeking selfish advancement without concern for the rest of our people, adopted European standards in a very artificial kind of way, telling the *bwana* what he liked to hear, standing as candidates for white Parties, and offering themselves as showpieces of the Partnership policy. They cut themselves off from the African people in order to qualify for membership of the élite white society, their ultimate fate was a sad one. Scorned by their own people, they were abandoned without compunction by their white patrons when they had outlived their usefulness and ended up in a kind of half world between the two racial groups, acceptable to neither.

Our sympathetic white citizens ought not to make the opposite error. We do not expect, as the price of indentification with our society, the abandonment of all that is a genuine part of their own culture. We recognise that Zambia will be all the richer for the wealth and variety of human types within it. It would be a very drab society indeed if all behaved and spoke identically. There is a distinctive contribution to be made by our white citizens and therefore there is no need for them to try to imitate us or demonstrate their fidelity by turning their backs upon their own people. We are not interested in white *Africans*; it is white *Zambians* we value—Europeans who are committed to our country and its future, loyal to our State, serving according to their gifts and providing a distinctive colour in the rich tapestry of our national life. Identification need not mean absolute uniformity.

The white citizens who have a sense of identification with our new society have the important task of acting as a bridge group, helping to allay the unreasonable fears of their fellow whites because they are in a position to speak from first-hand experience of colleagueship and friendship with black citizens.

We Africans who have been at the receiving end of the the colour bar know better than anyone that it is not possible for a man to change the colour of his skin. We do not expect our white citizens to make the attempt. Let them be what they are—relaxed and happy citizens of Zambia, not bad imitations of black Zambians.

*   *   *

I also believe that our white citizens can bring an independent and critical judgement to bear upon our national problems. There is much rubbish being talked and written about the sensitivity to criticism of the newly independent African states . . . press censorship, stifling of the opposition parties and so on, *ad infinitum*. Now make no mistake about it, national survival comes first. Africa is not Hyde Park Corner, where mob orators can propound any preposterous political philosophy in the happy knowledge that the public will not take them seriously. We are engaged in a life and death struggle to preserve national integrity and prevent fragmentation through regionalism and tribalism. It is our duty to maintain the strictest control over individuals or movements who may attempt to drive a wedge amongst our people and spread dissension and subversion. Of course, there is a certain type of criticism about which we are highly sensitive; that calculated to erode away the people's confidence in their leaders or to fan to life old antagonisms, or designed to weaken the State for the benefit of outside enemies. Nor do we take kindly to criticism directed at us from positions of comfortable remoteness from our struggle.

Having said that, let me add that we welcome the constructive criticisms of those who have identified themselves with us unreservedly. Any Zambian, whatever his colour, whose future and whose family's future are bound up in the nation's destiny, can criticise away for all he is worth, and provided he has something worth saying, our Government will listen. We have not got closed minds—we are too conscious of the slenderness of our resources and the magnitude of our problems. It is only from spectators we tend to resent constant barracking. The people who are afraid to get their feet wet have no right to tell us how to swim to shore. But if they are up to their necks in the torrent alongside us, then we welcome their viewpoint. I spend quite some time listening to the critical comments of Europeans whose integrity I respect. This is not to say that I accept or modify my policies in terms of such criticism. I must reserve the right to know, after due consultation with my colleagues, what is best for my own people. But I respect such constructively critical judgement and always take it into account.

But the essential prerequisite of such criticism must always be some degree of understanding of our African way of doing things. It is no use telling us that we ought to do something in a certain way because that is how Europeans always did it. I am not interested in the national origins of the solutions we adopt to our problems. If we endorse a policy, we do so because we think it is right and in the best interests of our people and not because that is how things are done in Britain or the United States, or Russia, or even in the old Northern Rhodesia.

The leader's first duty is to carry the people with him. The people are sovereign in Zambia. All our policies must, sooner or later, make sense to them, and, therefore, many worthwhile theoretical schemes are of no avail because our people would not be receptive to them.

*　　　　*　　　　*

I feel a word of warning is in order to our white supporters on the dangers of creating in their minds stereotypes of the African personality. The social psychologist tells us that stereotypes are mental pictures of another racial group to which strong emotion is attached. Insulting labels such as 'Wog', 'Nigger', 'Yid' are examples of such stereotypes. Some Europeans still see Africans as stereotypes rather than individuals, much to their confusion and our fury.

Now just as reactionary Whites tend to think in stereotypes about Africans, so occasionally do progressive Whites, though their mental images are always favourable rather than insulting. Nevertheless, they *are* stereotypes. They have mental images of us derived from the days of the freedom struggle; they expect us to behave as we did then. To put my point in personal terms. I am no longer the Ken of the old days, I am President of the Republic of Zambia. This does not mean, I hope, that I am now unapproachable or forgetful of old friends; you know that this is not true. But it does mean that there can be no presumption upon old friendships. I cannot afford to have favourites; I and my colleagues are responsible for the welfare of four million people. I am sure I do not need to labour this point. We do not expect uncritical adulation from our white supporters; neither can they expect from us favoured treatment. Our new and grinding responsibilities call for a reappraisal of old relationships in terms of an honesty and realism unobscured by false sentimentality about the past. I am sure I need not add that none of the foregoing is to suggest that we do not value and intend to keep in good repair long-standing friendships. But let there neither be disappointment nor disillusionment that the rigorous demands of the present may modify the old carefree relationships of the past.

*　　　*　　　*

If reactionary Whites tend to indulge themselves in prognostications of doom about the future of Zambia, progressive Whites must guard against the opposite danger —of superficial optimism, which when their dreams are not quickly realised, dissolves into despair.

Although some Europeans have been emotionally involved in our struggles and share fully our aims and purposes as a nation, they can never completely follow the inner logic of the African mind, and therefore they may underestimate the complexity of the peculiar problems which face us, or fail to appreciate fully the delicate balance of forces with which we have got to reckon. There is no reason why they should have this peculiar understanding. But it does mean that they must be extremely diffident about making slick judgements concerning our success or failure. In some cases I know their legitimate pride is involved because they have countered the negative arguments of our critics with confident assertions that miracles would be performed overnight once the Party attained power.

We are building for the ages in Africa. The State of Zambia must be strongly established in order to withstand the ravages of time. So it is futile to wring one's hands in despair if the whole structure does not go up at once. As a Party and as a Government our ultimate aims remain always the same, but we have to work against time, which may mean a concentration upon certain problems to the exclusion of others. It may sometimes appear to our White supporters that we are neglecting areas of urgency and emphasising the apparently secondary in our national planning. But they must remember that the nation of Zambia is in the last resort *people*, and human beings are not so easily manipulated as statistics or blueprints or development plans. They have wills of their own, hopes, dreams and fears, which must all be taken into account when priorities are decided. Much as we would like to vindicate the judgement of our European supporters against the jeers of their opponents, our first responsibility is not to make cheap and dramatic gestures but to establish painstakingly a national structure which is in no danger of collapse when strains and stresses are applied to it.

*　　　　*　　　　*

I was much interested in your comment about the need

to value the European sector of our society in terms of what they *are* rather than what they *do*. I would say that our people must achieve that maturity of judgement whereby they come to regard our European citizens not primarily as a *skill* but as a *presence*. And this will require considerable adjustment of our thinking. As you know, for many years European settlers enjoyed a monopoly of technical, professional and administrative skills. Indeed, this fact was always regarded as sufficient justification for their political and social dominance over the last half century. They were entitled, so the colonialist argument ran, to social privilege and a monopoly of political power because they had the skills without which a society could not function. European politicians waxed fat at election times on the bogey that African nationalism must be resisted because otherwise European skills would be frightened away from the country.

Hence the African mind has been conditioned historically to think of Europeans in terms of their usefulness, particularly in the upper echelons of industry, commerce, the professions and government. The basis of the European demand for special protection in the independence Constitution was the necessity for conserving their irreplaceable skills. So it is hardly surprising that our African citizens tend to have a very utilitarian judgement of their white fellow-citizens. And I would be the last to under-value the importance of their skills and competence to our nation. Nevertheless, the utilitarian valuation of people is not good for human relations, in that we must recognise that over and above what people can do, they make a contribution to our society merely by being there—a presence to be cherished for what they are. Otherwise, as our society becomes more sophisticated and the level of indigenous technical and academic attainment rises, Europeans will tend to be regarded as superfluous.

But no genuine group within a society can ever be judged superfluous to it or else there is something wrong with the values upon which that society is based. We would like our European citizens to feel that they are cherished for themselves and not merely because they happen to be doctors or engineers or scientists. I must of course add that I am not now thinking of European passengers amongst us who use their racial origins in order to retain privileges unrelated to contribution. Such people will find not only Zambia but most of the modern world increasingly unsympathetic to their racist thinking.

*   *   *

There are no substitutes for patience and forebearance in the attempts of Africans and Europeans to come to terms within the new society. We do not under-estimate the difficulties Europeans will face in adjusting to the bloodless revolution which brought about our independence. You cannot be for years a member of the 'master race' in Africa, no matter how impeccable your behaviour, without the evidences lingering in a tone of voice or a look in the eye. Where Europeans make the effort to achieve a new evaluation of their black fellow-citizens, they will find our people patient and forbearing. Equally, Europeans will be called upon to exercise forbearance in those isolated situations where they provoke, undeservedly, a sharp reaction from an African citizen. These incidents, which have been encouragingly rare, are more likely to be the results of the conditioning of the colonial era than deliberate malice. Both racial groups are at the moment incredibly sensitive—their nerves are on the outside of their skins and only time will heal the deep-seated wounds of the past. But Europeans who are prepared to fight their way through the problems of adjustment will be rewarded by receiving the African confidence and find a good, happy home for themselves and their families amongst us.

5

The Future of Nationalism

African nationalism, this explosive force which has changed the shape of the Continent, is a curious phenomenon. It was, I think, Lord Hailey who pointed out that there were originally few nations in Africa within which nationalist feeling could develop. Nationalism in Europe appears to have been basically concerned to unify people with a common language and culture—the growing awareness amongst people in a given geographical area that since they were a nation, it was time they behaved like one.

With the exception of certain traditional kingdoms such as Ashanti, Buganda, Barotse or Zulu, the basic unit in Africa appears to have been the tribe, which far from having a sense of oneness with its neighbours, often regarded them as mortal enemies. Nor has African nationalism always had the advantage of a common language and culture to act as cohesive factors to bind the people together. More often than not the task of evolving a common culture and language has only begun once the independence struggle is over. Nor, failing language and cultural unity, has there normally been one great religion such as Islam which could provide a focus of unity. Indeed, the opposite is often the case—religious divisions on the African continent have been a major cause of disunity and strife.

Because of these difficulties, Lord Hailey doubted whether

the term *nationalism* ought to be used at all for this political force, preferring the word *Africanism*. To my mind this is much too imprecise. I think *nationalism* is a legitimate term because it certainly describes the goal of all our activity if not the natural origins of our sense of solidarity. Our aim has been to create genuine nations from the sprawling artifacts the colonialists carved out all over the Continent.

*   *   *

Nationalism originated as a movement of protest. First intellectuals, then town-dwellers and finally whole populations rose up in protest against colonialism. In its early stages the nationalist movement was often little more than a 'talking shop' where intellectuals engaged in a certain amount of gentlemanly agitation in order to win the social recognition in a white élite society to which their education and culture entitled them. Then in the 'Congress' phase, a mass movement emerged as town-dwellers came up against the colour-bar and began to question the authority of the colonial overlord. In its Congress phase, the nationalist movement was more the concrete embodiment of political frustration and African solidarity than a political party in the strict sense, because few Africans had access to the ballot box. Only when significant numbers of Africans were given the vote, or failing this, the colonial power was relaxing its grip sufficiently to make non-constitutional activity possible, did African nationalism crystallise into political parties proper.

The economic and social forces which have had a decisive effect upon the shaping of the nationalist movement on its road towards its goal are many and various. The creation of a money economy resulted in large numbers of men being thrown together and brought into being the labour movements which are the handmaidens of nationalism in the freedom struggle. Urbanisation weakened traditional loyalties and created 'open' personalities, men available for a new kind of allegiance. Length of contact with the colonial power also had its effect. For this determined the number of educated Africans there were and the extent to which they could gain experience of the legislative process. The presence or otherwise of a white settler community capable of using political and economic weapons to slow up African advancement influenced the militancy of the developing nationalist movement. Most important of all possibly, was the policy of the colonial power—whether it was amenable to African advancement against pressure, which is the British pattern, or committed to suppressing completely the political aspirations of the African people, thus driving the nationalist movement underground and forcing it to achieve its goal by revolution as in the former Belgian Congo. Finally, tribal, regional and personal rivalries affected the speed at which the nationalist movement could achieve its jumping off point—mass solidarity in the freedom struggle.

Whatever combination of factors has influenced the development of African nationalism, the important question is this: what happens to nationalism as a movement of protest when the basic target of its protest—the colonial power— has been removed? The withdrawal of the colonial power, whilst solving one great problem, raises another equally acute for the nationalist leader. The discipline and solidarity of the national movement and the impetus built up during the freedom struggle are vital to the success and survival of the new nation. Yet unless new, exciting and worthwhile goals can be proposed for nationalism, there is danger of the movement of protest turning inwards upon itself and becoming destructive of the national good.

*   *   *

In one sentence, the nub of the nationalist leader's problem is *how can we transform nationalism into patriotism?* If we accept the Oxford Dictionary's definition of patriotism as 'a zealous love for one's country' then it follows in Africa that this is something which will have to be engendered, because until independence few Africans were aware in this sense that they had a country—their loyalties were more restricted and fragmentary. Independence does not usher into existence a mature nation—it is little more than the realisation of a dream which must then be clothed with reality.

The loyalties that nationalism calls into being are at once too general and too restricted to warrant being called patriotism. Its general aspect is the people's 'Africanness'— a sense of solidarity which transcends national boundaries, drawing sustenance from the struggles and victories of African leaders and their people all over the Continent. This emotional identification of the people with their brothers over the horizon, struggling, fighting and working, though admirable, is much too vague and wide-ranging a loyalty to form the basis of patriotism, which needs sharper, more defined objects. At the same time, the loyalty of the members of the nationalist movement may be too specific, being solely political in orientation. The vehicle of these sentiments of loyalty is the party, which marshals, channels and controls it. And the person of the leader provides a specially intense focus of loyalty. He is the people's mouth-piece. He suffers with them and on their behalf. They speak through his voice and he leads them where they have trusted him to take them.

The people's sense of identification in the struggle to achieve certain political goals is much too narrow to con-stitute patriotism, which demands a certain degree of loyalty to every element in the nation as well as one's comrades, and which must have social and cultural and religious elements as well as political. Nor is loyalty to the leader sufficient. For the new state, if it is to be healthy and well-founded, must outlast the life-time of any leader. It is the ultimate confession of failure when a state is unable to survive the death or eclipse of its leader and goes down in anarchy and factionalism. Every sound political institution must solve the problem of succession, ensure the peaceful transfer of political power from one party to another (should the people will it) and also provide for continuity of leadership. A leader can only prove his indispensability at the expense of his country's future.

And yet . . . the leader cannot afford to be too precipitate in diverting the people's loyalty from him for in many nationalist movements he is the lynch pin of unity. He has been chosen and has survived because he was able to hold in balance tribal, regional and personal factions; because the people had reason to believe that he would not be exercising his power in an arbitrary manner, favouring this group against that one, drawing his ministers from one area or tribe. The government of the independent African state is normally a masterpiece of compromise and delicate balance!

I know that a great volume of criticism is heaped upon the leaders of the new States of Africa because their image, after independence, far from waning, tends to assume superhuman proportions. Charges of fascism and messianism are common. But this type of criticism (except when applied to leaders who are obvious megalomaniacs) fails to take account of the crucial role of the leader in maintaining national unity. He is often the only fixed point in a rapidly changing and mentally confusing society. Any precipitate attempt to divert the loyalty of the people can result in their being left without any bearings whatever.

Without doubt, this lionisation puts a great strain on the character of the leader of a nationalist movement. He needs all his moral fibre to avoid the corrupting effects of great power. There must be a rationality about his policies and behaviour which make it clear to the humblest citizen that he acts not on the basis of masterful whim but as the servant of the state. I personally find that my religion is a useful antidote to any megalomanic tendencies I might develop. I never cease to remind both the people and myself that I am not a supreme potentate but a humble servant of Almighty God. I do not miss any opportunity in my public utterances of turning the people's eyes away from me towards God as the true sustainer and protector of the nation.

*   *   *

The problem of transforming nationalism into patriotism is particularly acute in those African States, such as Zambia, where the Head of State is also Leader of the Party as well. In any democracy, an executive head of state is involved in a delicate balancing act. As President, he must show absolute impartiality to colleagues and political opponents alike; he may not use his high office to gain political advantage or restrict unnecessarily the legitimate attempts of the opposition to unseat him. On the other hand, his continuance in office which, false modesty aside, he regards as essential for the good of the nation, depends upon his being able to maintain control of the Party and to strengthen its hold upon the allegiance of the people.

In newly established states without a long experience of working this system, it is not always easy to define just where the dividing line between legitimate opposition and sedition runs. It could also be claimed that this transformation of nationalism into patriotism is difficult of achievement when a sizeable minority representing the opposition are taught by their party leaders to view the President, not as the Head of State, but as the leader of a party they are pledged to overthrow at the polls.

Whilst I am alive to the dangers in combining the offices of Chief Executive and Head of State, I see no realistic alternative in Africa. For in the absence of a President with some historical or traditional claim to loyalty divorced from politics, there are great dangers in expecting a people whose loyalty has been channelled politically, to be able to show two kinds of loyalty to different personalities. In my view, if the leader is to direct the people's loyalty to the state over a period of time, he must first be in undisputed possession of it. The larger the number of personalities who have an absolute claim on the people's loyalty, the greater the possibility of tribal or regional divisions being intensified.

There is this too, to be said for the executive President; he is answerable to the people not only at election times, but can also keep in touch with their mood and thinking through those highly sensitive reflectors of public opinion, the party officials. These officials are in daily contact with the masses, and though they may show the appropriate degree of respect to the leader *qua* President, they are able to speak to him with the utmost frankness in his role as leader of the party. To travel as I do from State House to the Party Headquarters for a caucus meeting is a salutary experience. Behind closed doors the policies and actions of the President are ruthlessly analysed and the effects of those policies upon the people reported and assessed. Granted, there is the opposing danger that a President dependent upon political election may pander to public opinion, avoid unpopular policies, and try to give the people what they want rather than what they need. But there are no mechanical substitutes for integrity in a national leader. No system devised by man can compensate for moral cowardice and vacillation. Whilst understanding the concern of political scientists and theorists to evolve institutions of government which will neutralise any negative qualities in the Chief Executive, I still maintain that moral fibre and character are more important than any mechanisms of government in ensuring justice for all. Efficient systems of government may help prevent a good leader from making errors of judgement but they are powerless to stop a bad leader from using his great power to tyrannise his people either through malice or stupidity.

But the lesson of history seems to be that the people

sooner or later realise that the one they thought their shepherd is in fact a wolf and take the appropriate action. Lincoln was right in his claim that you cannot fool all the people all the time. The most costly mistake a leader can make is to underestimate the capacity of the people to appreciate that they are being duped.

*   *   *

Let me offer some further thoughts on the role of the leader in helping to transform nationalism into patriotism.

In the first place it is the leader's task to ensure continuity of public function by tackling the problem of succession to the high offices of the state. Hence he is constantly at work finding and encouraging suitable young men to accept ever-increasing responsibilities, assessing their capabilities, their honesty and their capacity for handling power. It must be borne in mind, of course, that a nation is not an inert, static thing. It is an organism which changes as it grows. So the leader's problem is not solely to ensure a supply of men with the correct qualities for high office in 1966, but also to predict what qualities are likely to be needed in ten or twenty years time. What will the Zambia of 1986 look like? What will its social pattern and economic shape be? Assuming that we are successful in our crusade to defeat the enemies of our immediate survival, what great challenges will face the nation in twenty-five years' time, and what skills and aptitudes will be required to answer them? Our present generation of leaders chose themselves in the sense that they came to prominence in the freedom struggle. They won their commissions on the battle-field. Our future leaders must be chosen without the advantage of such dramatic character tests as the battle for independence provides. Management theorists, I am told, devote a great amount of attention to the solution of the problem of succession in the industrial concern. But there, at least, they are required only to make predictions in the economic realm. In grooming the future leaders of a newly independent state, we have the much more daunting task of making predictions in an area where political, social and economic forces interact, and where the number of imponderables which history throws in for good measure are considerable.

But one mistake the wise leader will not make is to designate too early an heir apparent for his own position. This is a foolhardy thing to do, given the highly fluid state of politics in Africa; it is also the ultimate cruelty to the young man concerned, who would as a consequence excite the envy and spite of disappointed aspirants who might do everything possible to destroy him. In this matter, I believe that the will of the people is truly sovereign, and that the leader, for all his wide-ranging concerns, must not assume initiatives which ought to be left to them.

Secondly, the leader must recognise that politics alone do not create a nation; a whole network of cultural, religious and social factors play an important role. Nation-building, therefore, is not solely a political operation, active encouragement must also be given to the development of drama, poetry, literature, art, sport and every other activity through which the spirit of the people expresses itself. A nation held together only by political forces is a drab barracks of a place, and more than this, such links are transient. For it is of the essence of politics that things change, whereas a nation must have a framework which does not collapse whenever radical political change occurs.

I am often chided by my friends, concerned for my health, about the amount of time I give to attending functions which they regard as minor aspects of the nation's life. Hoard your energy they plead, for the great areas of political decision-taking and let one of your subordinates do the honours at these cultural occasions. But for me, a YMCA function, a Church service, an Arts Festival or a football match are not minor aspects of the nation's life. They are arteries through which the vital fluid of nationhood flows. Zambia's first original contribution to the world's music, art or literature, our first international sports star or entertainer, will be landmarks of nationhood as momentous as a mighty dam, a modern airline or an international highway.

The will of our people is expressed through the political channel, but their soul shines through their culture. May I quote at you some of your own words:

Nationalism is not enough. Healthy nations cannot be built upon mass allegiances. The people must be integrated into smaller and more concrete social units than the national movement. The only firm foundation of the nation is a network of interlocking relationships at the grass roots, beginning with the family, stretching outwards through local associations to the larger community.*

The protection and extension of national symbols is of paramount importance in stimulating patriotism. I do not necessarily find all the ceremonial which attaches to my office as Head of State congenial to me. But I am aware that the Office of the Presidency is a focus of patriotic sentiment. So I heartily approve of bills passed in our Parliament making it an offence to show disrespect to the Person of the President, the National Anthem or our National Flag. I get no egotistic satisfaction when such laws are invoked. One of the burdens of leadership is that a fallible human being must accept as though it were his right a degree of adulation and respect of which he feels unworthy. But it has got to be done, and indeed the President must be most punctilious in accepting the dignity of his office; for what he treats lightly, he can hardly expect the people to take seriously.

Time magazine recently made the odd comment that whenever I happen to hear the National Anthem played on the radio at close-down, I leap out of bed and stand to attention! This may be journalistic licence, but I am not

* Colin Morris, *Church and Challenge in a New Africa*. Epworth, 1964, p. 155.

ashamed to confess that in normal circumstances I do stand to attention and warm with pride when I hear our National Anthem played, for it serves to remind me of the miracle of our nationhood and the truth that I, and the humblest Zambian who hears that inspiring melody, are both servants of a cause greater than ourselves. This heartstirring we feel when the National Anthem is played is a first symptom of the transformation of nationalism into patriotism. Nationalism can inspire men to struggle, and if necessary, to die for a great cause, but patriotism alone will enable them to live for it.

The young people of our nation must be the special target for the encouragement of patriotic sentiment. A generation is now arising which has only the dimmest memory of colonialism, and soon the freedom struggle will be a matter for the history books. Hence we must in school instil into them a degree of national sentiment which will make them proud to be citizens of Zambia. Without becoming parochial and isolationist in our approach to education, we must put such emphasis upon our own history, geography, customs and art as will make them conscious of the land to which they belong. I am always intensely moved when I see the children of a little village school in some remote part of the country drawn up under the flagpole, raising the flag and singing the National Anthem as their first act of the day. With any luck, this generation will think of itself not in tribal terms as Bemba, Lozi or Tonga, but as Zambians. This is the only guarantee of our future stability. I know that there is a great abhorrence in certain circles in Britain and elsewhere of what is called the 'indoctrination' of schoolchildren. Such critics, besides their ignorance of the problems of a newly established State, must also have the dimmest memories of their own childhood. What is History to the British or Americans but the long and glorious tale of their great heroes, mighty battles and outstanding achievements? No true patriot could teach history without, however unconsciously, glorifying his own kith and kin. All education is indoctrination—the selection of certain themes and ideas from amongst the limitless accumulation of human knowledge which reflect certain truths that the educators regard as important. We make no apology for the fact that we intend to indoctrinate our children in the glories of Zambia and the privileges of being citizens of Africa. Providing the spirit of free enquiry and the critical faculty is not impaired, we believe that nothing but good can come from moulding the child's mind in such a way as to make him a useful and constructive citizen of our future society.

This inculcation of respect for authority and the protection of national symbols is of crucial importance because it is necessary to reverse a trend of the pre-independence period. It was necessary for nationalist leaders to encourage civil disobedience during the freedom struggle. The police and authorities were defied; at times we were not able to show the respect due to the Governor as Representative of the Crown. We pursued this policy, not because we are at heart a disrespectful people, but because we could not accept the moral basis of the authority of the Colonial Power. Now we have to take vigorous steps to ensure that we do not become victims of our own strategy. Contempt for the police and disregard of lawful authority can become a habit. Now that the authority reflects the expressed will of our people and the police are the instruments of that authority, the trend must be reversed by education and propaganda. But this is just one example of the kind of problem not uncommon in the West where the behaviour appropriate to one situation becomes dangerous when circumstances change . . . teaching men to kill in war-time is one example.

The nationalist party itself plays a formative role in the creation of patriotic sentiment. Because of its size and high degree of organisation, it touches the lives of the masses at many points. It is a structure of communication and control. But no longer must it be seen in post-independence days as the repository of the people's ultimate loyalty as was the case during the freedom struggle. It has got to engage in such constructive nation-building activity as will show it to be a servant-organisation of the State. For this reason, my own party has an extensive educational programme, offering bursaries to promising students, running schools for uneducated women, organising co-operatives, engaging in road building projects. In recent times, party officials have thrown their weight behind Government campaigns, to encourage mass vaccination, to give blood, stamp out mosquitoes and so on. Party training courses for stenographers and administrators have helped to build up a reservoir of skills upon which Government can draw. In such ways, the party is teaching the lesson that politics is not an end in itself but a powerful force in nation-building. At election time, we may pay the penalty for all this non-political activity in which the Party has been absorbed to the neglect of political agitation and propaganda. But in this, as in all else, the nation comes first.

*   *   *

Let me turn to the role of the intellectual in nationalist politics, since this group will be increasingly influential in directing the future course of nationalism.

By intellectual, I mean anyone who has a level of modern education beyond that of the mass of the people and who is prepared to become politically involved. The intellectual must be distinguished from the academic who is not a man of action but dedicated to the disinterested pursuit of knowledge for its own sake. He must also be distinguished from the scholar who is versed in traditional lore—the Confucian scholar in China, the Islamic scholar in the Middle East or the tribal elder in Africa. The intellectual is essentially an engaged man, applying modern knowledge and training to political purposes.

The intellectual group has been a key element in most twentieth-century revolutions, particularly in Africa. As I have explained earlier, nationalism often began as a revolt of intellectuals who, frustrated in their attempts to break into the white élite societies, turned back to their own people and became the spear-heads of the movement for political emancipation.

The task of leading nationalist movement devolves in most cases upon intellectuals because there was no other group within society to throw up leaders. The traditional, hereditary leaders such as chiefs had become tainted through the deliberate policy of the colonialists in using them as the agents of indirect rule. And indeed many traditional rulers, far from welcoming the rise of nationalism, saw it as a focus of an alternative form of power within African society and as a threat to their own supremacy. And what other leaders did the African people have? In Central Africa at least, there were no indigenous military élites—the armed forces were white-officered and other ranks were rendered politically impotent. So the onus of marshalling the people, working out strategy and leading agitation fell upon a small minority of teachers, lawyers, doctors, journalists and sometimes clergymen.

Often the economic and social colour bar drove intellectuals into politics because all doors to advancement in their own professions were shut. The nationalist party as it grew in strength and influence could absorb all these workless intellectuals at national, regional or local levels. The party in pre-independence days fulfilled the function taken over by Government once independence had been won—that of being the major employer of African intellectuals.

As political consciousness grew and the freedom struggle intensified, young intellectuals were attracted to the cause in their student days. The student tends to be a natural rebel, orientated against authority and sharpening his wits by challenging those responsible for his education. It seems to me that the highly misguided attempt by the Rhodesia Government in 1965 to fence students off from politics by making it a condition of receiving a government grant that students should not be engaged in nationalist politics was the ultimate in stupidity. The student is radical by training and temperament. Close off all channels for the legitimate political expression of this radicalism and you are inviting him to become a revolutionary as was the case under the Kuomintang régime in China, where students were driven into the arms of Communism through such restrictive measures.

Temperamentally, the intellectual was attracted to nationalism because neither colonialism nor tribalism would allow him scope for the exercise of that critical faculty which is the most precious fruit of his training. Any intellectual employed by a colonial government had to pay the price of supine acceptance of their policies as a condition of employment. To show too independent a turn of mind was to invite dismissal. No less rigid was the tribal authority. To be seen flirting with any known nationalists would lead to social ostracism and loss of employment. So in the struggle which always rages between nationalism and tribal authority in the early stages of the freedom fight, the intellectual found that he could not, in all honesty, accept the basis of traditional authority or the obscurantism of those who were prepared to see the masses languish under colonial rule in order to secure their own limited authority.

Literacy is the most powerful weapon in the nationalist's armoury. Therefore, the intellectual also rose to prominence in the political movements because he had a grasp of the colonial language—English, French or Portuguese—which had inevitably become the language of politics. In former British territories, the Legislature's proceedings were carried on and reported in English, the main newspapers, the political textbooks, the pamphlets, the international news were all expressed in English. The leader fluent only in a vernacular, though well able to marshal the masses and put across to them his ideas, was cut off from the main flow of political ideas and events. He was unable to encounter the colonial power in debate and dialogue or move in the larger international world of politics. So he gave place to the intellectual.

Colonialists were well aware of the power of indigenous intellectuals and tried to apply a 'divide and rule' policy towards them, patronising and advancing them within narrow limits, so cutting them off from their own people in the hope of rendering the nationalist movement impotent. The Republic of South Africa has become over many years a past master at this game of trying to make the interests of the intellectuals at least economically identical with those of the white communities, in the hope that they would see the political advancement of the masses as a threat rather than an advantage. Many of the African intellectuals who were founders of the African National Congress of South Africa were politically destroyed because they became tainted with this touch of white patronage. Certainly it took strong-mindedness on the part of any intellectual to turn his back upon economic advantage in order to stand shoulder to shoulder with his own people. One of the most serious charges to be laid at the door of the colonialists is that they practised the morally suspect philosophy of appealing to self-interest on the part of the tiny group who had won for themselves an education in order to cut them off from their own people who needed their help and leadership.

The speed with which African territories won their independence in the post-war world caught many intellectuals off balance. There had grown up on the West Coast of Africa comparatively large classes of intellectuals well-established in their chosen professions when the freedom struggle hotted up. But in Central Africa, the educational system under colonialism had been so poor that we had not the advantage of the stabilising influence of mature professional men. The ridiculously small number of Africans who had managed to fight their way to university entrance standard were of such recent vintage that the freedom struggle caught them in the midst of their studies for professional qualifications. They were in an agonising dilemma. On the one hand they were emotionally involved in the struggle of the masses for freedom and dearly wished to join in; on the other they were far-sighted enough to realise that once the dust settled and the battle was over we should need every professionally qualified African we could find to replace the departing colonialists. What were they to do? I often found myself in the position of giving advice to such advanced students, and I always counselled them to press ahead with their training and prepare themselves for gigantic challenges when independence was won. To win our independence of the colonialists and then have to remain abjectly dependent upon them to supply all the nation's professional and technical skills would be to reduce freedom to a farce. But I also warned them against becoming so Western-orientated during their study periods abroad that they would no longer be along the wavelength of the masses when they returned. Experience also led me to alert them to the many attempts which would be made to seduce their minds and enlist them in the cause of some ideology which was not in our country's best interests. I assured them that they would be engaging in their own subtle freedom struggle whilst abroad against enemies of Africa's neutrality.

I have learned that the moral law of this Universe is so delicately balanced that one rarely enjoys advantages without also suffering penalties. This first generation of pre-independence intellectuals who were occupied with their studies whilst the freedom struggle raged at home incurred the envy and disgruntlement of some of the ordinary people who made great sacrifices in the cause of freedom. To these freedom fighters, the intellectuals who had apparently luxuriated in London or New York whilst the battle was at its hottest were rewarded on their return by important and well-paid posts in the government on the strength of educational qualifications others had to forego, except for what reading they could manage in a prison cell or detention camp. Here is a lively source of tension within the nationalist movement following independence. I want to go into greater detail about this later.

*   *   *

When the freedom struggle is over and independence is assured, the intellectual reaps a rich reward. A whole range of government, administrative and professional posts become available to him. He is a favoured son of the revolution. But there is not necessarily room at the top for all the intellectuals in the nationalist movement. Some suffer disappointment as their expectations are frustrated. In their disgruntlement, such aggrieved intellectuals can easily become threats to national unity. They are the ones who can be expected to flirt with ideologies such as Communism, because they know that they will never command sufficient popular support to realise their ambitions. They seek outside help to dislodge their former comrades in power. The intellectual committed to the work of nation-building is one of the country's greatest assets. The intellectual standing aside in pique because he has not received the recognition he feels is due to him is a very dangerous man indeed.

Nor is life always easy for the intellectuals who have been given posts of responsibility, for they are often somewhat tender plants unless toughened in the freedom struggle. They see government in academic, rational terms as they have been taught. They are prone to disillusionment when their neat theories do not work out so tidily on the ground; when they strike all the snags involved not in finding answers but in motivating people. Your freedom fighter on the other hand, much of whose adult life has been spent in motivating people through political tactics, is not so prone to disillusionment. He knows what discouragement means. He has seen many false starts, suffered many defeats. He has great respect for the surprising, unpredictable human material which is the object of all government.

For the Party, the loss of its intellectuals to wider responsibilities constitutes a crisis. Where, before, the nationalist movement offered unlimited scope for the employment of intellectuals, it is now the government and the wider society that affords the glittering opportunities—higher salaries and social prestige. The party politician, unless he is a government minister, loses a certain amount of status following independence. Party politics tend to languish in a backwater as the dramatic work of nation-building holds the spotlight. Yet it is vital to maintain and even improve the intellectual tone of the party for under the crash educational programmes of the independent government, the general level of academic attainment throughout the country rises rapidly. Unless party officials can keep abreast of this swelling educational tide, unless they can match the quick wits of the nation's young men, the party's hold upon the people will slowly relax and new formations come into being. It might be claimed that intellectuals in government posts are still party officials able to do a certain amount of political organisation in their spare time. But every ministry in the government of a newly independent state is snowed under by urgent and complex problems. An eighteen-hour working day is standard amongst the members of my own Cabinet. Apart from brief visits of top personalities to outlying areas, all the work on the ground devolves upon regional and local officials, and what they are unable to do does not get done at all.

In order to employ intellectual skills within the Party and to keep all officials on their toes, I have found it essential to use party machinery to shadow the thinking and planning of the government. Regional and local committees are given practical problems to solve; ministers present to them the fruits of their planning and consult them on how best to mobilise the people to give effect to these policies. At all costs the mental stagnation of the party between elections must be prevented.

*   *   *

I take your point that there is a distinction between the disgruntled intellectual whom personal spite has driven into opposition and the uncommitted intellectual who, from a position of independence of Government responsibility, stands for the flow of free ideas throughout society. Certainly the vast majority of the country's intellectuals under the pressure of government responsibility inevitably become specialists, concerned with one small area of the nation's life, and even then with day to day problems rather than long range planning. We need the uncommitted intellectual whose mind is able to range widely and to occupy himself with ideas which though not immediately germane to the business of nation-building stimulate free thought and dialogue on every matter of human concern. I would expect such cross-fertilisation of ideas to come from two directions, our institutions of higher learning and the Churches. In particular, the Ministry of the Churches comprises the largest single group of uncommitted intellectuals, charged by the Gospel they proclaim to deal with ultimate questions and by definition required to see society in the widest possible context—against the unchanging Laws of God. Let me be frank and state that I am disappointed in the failure of the clergy, with certain exceptions, to discharge this prophetic function. Is not a disproportionate amount of their time and intellectual talent solely devoted to matters of domestic ecclesiastical concern? Would it be unkind of me to say that many of the clergy have completely shut themselves off from the ongoing life of our nation and argue endlessly about the jot and tittle of the Law; theological niceties equally irrelevant to the salvation of the individual soul and the soul of the society? As a humble Christian, I am saddened that so much of the Church's intellectual talent is unavailable to stimulate and challenge our society. Both our Government and nation need to have kept before them the moral and spiritual standards against which we should measure our policies and actions. But we want only the best the Church is capable of giving us, not tired clichés or parrot-like repetition which are an insult to our intelligence. Never has the Church had a more wonderful opportunity to be a relevant and effective spiritual and moral force than it has in these newly established States where men are hungry for the truth. But the tragedy is that many of the uncommitted intellectuals in the Church are also unengaged; their talents and time turned inwards upon their own life, giving the impression of a Christian Church which is a powerful engine, running at top speed, but driving nothing.

*   *   *

I want to revert to this vexed question of the relationship between the intellectual and the freedom fighter in the nationalist movement. Failure to achieve a harmonious relationship between these two key elements in the party can tear it apart and has even rocked some Governments in Africa to their foundations.

As I have stated earlier, some intellectuals were also freedom fighters, but I am thinking particularly now of the intellectuals who were studying abroad during the crucial stages of the freedom struggle and who have only emerged to take prominent roles within the Party and Government since the advent of independence.

The cause of this tension is obvious. Your freedom fighter is a man, who whilst possibly possessing keen intelligence, sacrificed any hope of academic attainment in order to lead the people in the struggle. His fate and that of the intellectual were often markedly different during the battle for independence. Whilst the foreign-trained intellectual enjoyed the freedom of the university campus, the freedom fighter may have languished in gaol. Whilst the intellectual was being lionised in a foreign university world, the freedom fighter was on the run, persecuted, hunted down, often without any settled place to live.

Human nature being what it is, mutual resentment is easily aroused amongst these two groups. The freedom fighter may be jealous of the ease with which the intellectual wins high position without personal sacrifice; the intellectual may resent the popularity of the freedom fighter and look down upon him as unsophisticated and unfitted for high office.

The leader who genuinely values the contribution which both the intellectual and the freedom fighter can make to the nation is in a dilemma for he must try to harmonise their conflicting claims to office. In Zambia I have been fortunate in my colleagues, for these two groups within the party have achieved a remarkable degree of unanimity. Nevertheless, the possibility of friction is always there.

One of the roots of the problem is the obvious fact that the combination of skills and temperament which fit a man to lead the people into battle are not necessarily those which best equip him for administrative responsibility after victory has been won. Indeed, the temperament which produces the mob orator and the audacity which enables him to discount great odds and soldier on can become handicaps rather than advantages when times change. The freedom fighter naturally expects his reward and the people expect him to be rewarded. But to load him with responsibilities for which he is unsuited and which will break his heart is both cruelty to him and a disservice to the country.

Of course the fact that a man has been a freedom fighter rather than a cloistered intellectual in no way disqualifies him for high office. Some of the most competent of the Government leaders of the new Africa have come from the ranks of the freedom fighters. But the leader dare not forget that the people have elected him to safeguard their welfare, and this means that he cannot allow sentiment towards these brave and dedicated men to cloud his judgement about the best kind of Government which will serve the people. It is more important to assemble an efficient and well qualified team than to reward faithful party servants. If this requires the intellectual being favoured at the expense of the freedom fighter, then, however regretfully, this must be done.

In practice I have discovered that it is possible to blend the mentalities of freedom fighter and intellectual within a government in such a way as to reinforce their strengths and neutralise their weaknesses, providing the leader himself can bridge the gap between them in understanding and insight. For each brings his own distinctive contribution to the work of Government. The intellectual has a trained, analytical mind, he can probe a problem and assess priorities with a great degree of impartiality. He speaks the international language of government and can feed the results of his reading and research into cabinet debate. He is also less likely to be overawed by the technical accomplishment of his civil servants who will not find it easy to blind him with science.

The freedom fighter, on the other hand, is highly sensitive to the reaction of the ordinary people. He knows from experience how fast they can be driven, and he has a sympathy with their lot which comes from having lived on a miserable pittance and seen his family go without the good things of life. Possibly the freedom fighter's great asset is his ability to communicate with the people. Having dramatised the issues involved in the freedom struggle and motivated the people to act and suffer together, he is the ideal man to put across Government policy in colourful and simple language and to stir them to the work of nation-building.

Whereas the genuine intellectual tends to be Western-orientated, the freedom fighter often has his roots in traditional Africa. Each is prone to see a future society taking shape according to their own experience. Providing their debate does not develop into personal antagonism, some kind of equilibrium is achieved between the claims of the traditional and of the modern as elements in the new society through their joint presence in Government.

In striking this equilibrium, it is fatal for the leader to show a predilection for the one group at the expense of the other. He must be able to value and assess their contribution objectively, neither swayed by his admiration for the freedom fighter nor intimidated by the trained mind of the intellectual. It does no harm if both freedom fighters and intellectuals claim that the leader belongs to their camp, providing he is not demonstrably aligned with one rather than the other.

The problem of the freedom fighter versus intellectual is essentially a one-generation headache, for as the years wear on, Government will become increasingly intellectualised and freedom fighters will hold a hallowed niche in the nation's history but will no longer be a coherent group within the nationalist movement. But that element which the freedom fighter did provide; the distinctive flavour he brought to the work of Government must not be lost. There will always be a great need of men who can dramatise the struggle against the new enemies of freedom, poverty, ignorance and disease, and who can inspire the masses to turn to and defeat them.

*　　　　*　　　　*

African nationalism has, in our own country, achieved its primary purpose—liberation from colonialism and the generation of a certain amount of momentum to carry forward the work of building a sovereign nation. When we ponder the future of the movement, it is imperative to avoid the error of some theorists who talk of nationalism as though it had an independent existence as a force apart from the people who comprise it. Nationalism is not some

vibration in the ether, it is *people*, organised for given purposes, motivated towards certain goals and sharing certain
emotions and fears. We must therefore expect a regrouping
of the people as our nation begins to stratify in social classes,
with new élites springing up and political interests diversify-
ing. This is not to imply that the nationalist Party will
necessarily disappear but with the increasing sophistication
of the masses of our people it will certainly be transformed,
taking one of two directions. Either it will command such
widespread allegiance from the masses that we shall have a
de facto one-party state or else a multiplicity of political
parties will come into existence to represent sectional
interests. My own personal view is that the former is the
more likely. I confidently expect to see the virtual obliteration of the opposition at the next General Election, not by
draconian repressive measures, but through that 'painless
killer'—the ballot box. Then the nationalist movement will
be involved in massive reorganisation and structural changes
to ensure that the democratic process of free debate and
exchange which formerly occurred across the floor of the
Legislature is even more firmly institutionalised within the
governing party itself.

It would be truly tragic, however, if the spirit which
animated nationalists during the freedom struggle—their
brotherhood, courage and sacrifice, were lost to the life of
the nation. Such qualities won our freedom. They are badly
needed now to secure that freedom and give it substance.

*   *   *

I thought my reference to the one-party state would get a
rise out of you! I know that anyone conditioned to the democratic system as it operates in Great Britain or the
United States tends to detect an ominous undertone in the
very sound of the term. But if we are to make sense of
contemporary Africa, we must escape from the strait-
jacket of our preconceptions and have the charity to assume

that where the political systems of African States diverge from those of the ex-metropolitan power this is not necessarily due to pique or hunger for novelty; it may be that we have our own ideas about what is best for our people.

The trouble is that Britain exported to the African continent the Westminster Model, a system refined and polished over many centuries, and is utterly unable to believe that any sane African Government would wish to deviate from it. But difficult though it may be for devotees of the Westminster system to swallow the fact, the truth is that the Westminster Model is not so much the finest flower of democratic systems as a beautiful anachronism—a pattern ideally suited to the genius of the British people but of limited value, without drastic modifications, in modern Africa.

Throughout the twentieth century, the evolution of democracy has been away from the Westminster Model and towards strong centralised government, with power concentrated at the centre—the People's democracies of the Eastern bloc, military dictatorship in the Middle East and South America, the one-party State in Africa. Indeed, the pattern could well be summarised as authoritarian rule by popular consent. But to make the value judgement that this system is *ipso facto* totalitarian is unwarranted. There are ways that critical judgement of the ruling party's policies and free debate can be institutionalised other than by a multiplicity of political parties occupying the Legislature.

Let me mention some of the factors which have led independent African States to move away from the Westminster Model imposed upon them in the closing stages of colonial rule to the one-party system. In the first place, most liberation movements have enjoyed the overwhelming support of the people—in former British territories this was often the most important criterion by which the British Government decided when the time had come to withdraw. Was there a well-organised nationalist movement able to command mass support and with undisputed leadership?

Hence, many one-party States are the natural consequence of this process. The mass of the people supported one party and was prepared to trust that party with the task of guiding the new nation. In such circumstances, why on earth should leaders enjoying mass support artificially create an Opposition solely to accommodate those theorists who regard a government-in-waiting as essential to the democratic process? In many African States there is no opposition group worthy of the title 'Government-in-Waiting'. Generally the opposition does not present the country with a viable alternative to the government in power but is rather a rag-bag of disgruntled individuals and tribalists. My own personal view is that a *de facto* one-party state is preferable to that entrenched in the constitution or perpetuated by rigging the electoral arrangements in one's own favour. Democracy is first, last and all the time sovereignty of the people, or it is nothing. If the people have such confidence in a particular party that they give it an overwhelming majority at the polls then the best possible power-structure has been created for mobilising national resources for nation-building.

Another indication for a one-party system is that in Africa the things which divide contending groups tend to be of such fundamental significance that continuity of government could hardly be achieved through a change in the party in power. In countries such as Britain there is broad agreement on what might be termed political values. Methods of achieving these agreed goals differ and are set out in the party platforms. On the African continent, however, the historical causes of division tend to be so deep-seated that the very foundations of the State could be torn out if an opposition group were given too much latitude to inflame opinion. Hard though it may sound, in my view survival is more important than freedom of expression. The situation of near anarchy created in the recent past in such territories as the Congo, the Sudan and Pakistan through a multiplicity of weak political parties is a moral to us all. For a nation can flourish and its people benefit under strong government but anarchy is the basic denial of freedom because every aspect of the nation's life is paralysed. National survival is the basic good; all other qualities such as unlimited freedom of expression are contingent upon it. The great enemy of freedom is not totalitarianism but chaos.

Someone once wrote that in independent African States, the opposition tended either to be in gaol or in government. This is a pithy way of saying that the idea of an institutional Opposition is foreign to the African tradition. In our original societies we operated by consensus. An issue was talked out in solemn conclave until such time as general agreement could be achieved. The decision was then binding upon all the parties and it was a major sin against society for any of those who were privy to the decision to continue their agitation against it. The functions of a responsible Opposition are not always understood; rejection of a government measure can easily degenerate into a conspiracy to remove the government. The very solidarity of the support enjoyed by a national leader can become an invitation to Opposition groups to go beyond the law and use violence, assassination and sedition to destroy him. What leader in his right mind would allow such groups untrammelled freedom to mislead the public and rally disgruntled elements to their banner?

When a state of war exists, all nations restrict certain freedoms in the interests of national survival. The new States of Africa are in such a condition of national mobilisation. They are at war against terrible though impersonal enemies. There is not time for endless debate and arguing. Decisions have to be taken quickly and decisively. Inevitably, therefore, the Legislature ceases to be the major focus of power. It is not unimportant as a forum of national debate and a sounding board of public opinion. But most leaders in the new Africa find themselves having to take initiatives and formulate policies which in the older societies of the

West would emerge from the somewhat leisurely process of parliamentary debate.

I would repeat my contention that the soundest basis for a one-party state is the obliteration of the opposition through the ballot box, but I would also not deny that a government freely elected may find it necessary to hold a more rigorous view of personal liberty than is the case in the West. Paradoxical though it may seem, I believe that men may be truly free when serving a dedicated nation which in the interests of survival has to control to a certain extent their freedom of expression. Surely it is possible to combine freedom and obedience? The hard facts of life in modern Africa will only yield before the efforts of men who are prepared to make a willing response to the challenge of desperate necessity; who will make what has to be done the thing they want to do.

When all has been said about totalitarianism on the African continent, I refuse to believe that the indolent Westerner, who luxuriates in the possession of personal liberties which he rarely uses, is any more free than the authoritarian-directed African conscripted to answer challenges to his nation's survival.

*　　　　*　　　　*

A glance at this morning's newspaper suggests that a word about military coups in Africa is in order! It is much too early to make detailed comments on the particular coups reported (Nigeria and Ghana) but I certainly have views on the desirability of military government as such. Frankly I am opposed to it, though it is easy to see how the possibility arises. In many newly established states, the army is the best disciplined and most highly organised institution within the the nation. Certainly it has the most effective means of physical coercion. The soldiery are conditioned to obey orders without debate, argument and analysis—decisive mass action is, therefore, easily achieved.

It is also a characteristic of certain army leaders that their ambitions, fired by a rapid rise to eminence when colonial officers depart, cannot be contained within the military sphere. They tend to be impatient of politicians as anyone who reads Sir Winston Churchill's war memoirs will readily allow. It must too be difficult to resist the development of a grandeur delusion when you are aware that thousands of men await your every command, according you great deference and offering no resistance to your every whim.

Often the army is able to achieve a unity across tribal and regional divisions amongst its ranks much quicker than the politicians who, if they are to build a healthy nation, must reconcile differences rather than repress them. For this reason, an army may see itself as the ideal instrument for the creation of a uniform administration throughout the country. Well armed and well fed soldiers may scorn the civilian masses and deny their ability to participate in government.

But, to my mind, military government is always bad government. There are whole areas of the nation's life where a government, conscious of the deep feelings of the people, must desist from the use of the power at its disposal in order to persuade. Education rather than coercion is the only way in which certain national goals can be achieved. Military government has only one tactic—the unquestioning use of physical force. And for a government's image to appear before the people primarily as an authoritarian agency is bad for morale and poor education in democracy. The deference which is given to army officers is not evoked by their personal qualities however fine; it is respect paid to them in their capacity as servants of the state; it is the people acknowledging the sovereignty of the state through them by virtue of a commission granted to them to discharge certain functions. When those whose authority is vested in their servanthood become masters, the moral basis of Government is discredited.

With certain brilliant exceptions, the military mind is not

adept at the arts of politics. It knows little of the compromises, accommodations and persuasion which underlie political decisions. Because the military leader must have an unquestioning conviction that he knows what is best for those under him, he is prone to translate this possibly unwarranted self-confidence into the political sphere with disastrous results, for there are no representative mechanisms through which he can be curbed. Every political leader can be removed by due process of the constitution. He must always be keenly aware of the power of the people to dismiss him. The authority of the military leader is derived from sources other than public accountability and so he is likely to foment more trouble than he believes he has taken over power to settle.

Military power is always negative in character. There may be circumstances where widespread corruption justifies a military coup. But the most the army can do is to ensure basic law and order. It has not the means, the skill or the mandate to achieve detailed political reform.

Any Government established by military force is inviting its overthrow by the same means. God forfend that Africa should see a succession of revolutions and counter-revolutions of the kind which have scarred the face of the Middle East and Latin America.

The organisers of recent military coups in Africa have declared their intention of handing back power as soon as possible to the civil authorities. I pray that they do so at the first possible moment. Meanwhile, the moral of these coups must be taken to heart by all leaders in Africa. Corruption or complacency, degeneration of the nationalist Party, increasing remoteness of Governments from the people all invite this swift retribution. But let no one imagine that military coups are the final answer. The onward progress of the nation will be retarded and forces set in motion which inhibit that respect for democracy which is the essential prerequisite of all nation-building.

6

Towards Unity in Africa

I have become totally impervious to the sneers of those cynics who deride the avowed aim of most nationalist leaders—ever-closer links between sovereign African States until unified action in a variety of fields, economic, defence and foreign policy, is achieved. It is extraordinary that we are condemned for not achieving in less than twenty-five years what Europe has not yet been able to do (voluntarily) for the whole of its history. The existence of the Brazzaville, Monrovia and Casablanca blocs is pointed to as the death of our ideal, and we are asked to come to terms with the hard reality of history, learned long ago on other continents, that peoples *like* to remain apart; that national self-interest is the strongest force at work in our world.

Certainly, we need no outside observers to underline the difficulties in the way of continental unity. The facts of geography can be cited—the natural barriers Nature appears to have erected to keep us apart—the Sahara Desert dividing North Africa from the West and South; great ranges of mountains separating the West from the East. I am frankly not impressed by this argument. Australia has its vast deserts; it also has political unity. Both the United States and the Soviet Union are bisected by mountain ranges; they have achieved political unity. And the facts of geography could also work in our favour. More than a dozen of the new States of Africa are landlocked. They have no outlet to the sea. Hence, they will need to establish links with neighbours and set up arrangements for importing and exporting goods and for travel. The sinews of unity could well be uncovered in the hard facts of geography. It is not easy for a landlocked nation to pursue an isolationist policy!

It would be foolish too, to underestimate the great contrasts between African States, their widely divergent traditions and cultures, the eight hundred languages of the Continent, the varying political systems, the disparity between economic structures. And there is the legacy of that series of lines on the map drawn by the colonial powers who carved up Africa, often in defiance of or ignorance of ethnic and tribal realities; boundaries which are now a lively cause of dispute, as for example between Algeria and Morocco, Kenya and Somalia, Cameroon and Nigeria.

Yet granted all these difficulties, I believe it true to say that there is more genuine internationalist thinking in Africa than on any other continent in the world, and the desire to avoid 'balkanisation' is widely shared. Our conviction is not only widespread throughout the Continent; it is also urgent. Well-meaning observers often advise us to shelve our ambitions about wider unity until our national states are strongly established. When you have solved the major problems within your borders, they claim, you can then begin planning larger groupings.

I think this advice, though well-intentioned, is misleading. It takes account neither of psychological nor economic factors which indicate that the sooner we press forward towards our ultimate goal the better.

The psychological reason is this. Our nations are so new that the people have not yet had time to develop those rigid attitudes towards 'foreigners' which are characteristic of Europe. Clear-cut stereotypes about our neighbours have not taken possession of our minds, nor have we yet built up a history of division whereby our national pride demands that we resist the claims of other nations lest we be considered weak and appeasement-prone. It is not a matter of honour for us to prove that anything our neighbours can do, we can do better. The minds of our people are still malleable. They may well be more amenable to the sacrifices which wider links will demand at this moment than in twenty-five years' time.

Consider too, the often-quoted fact of Africa's so-called under-population. Whilst it may well be true that on the crudest possible estimate—number of bodies compared with total land-area—Africa is under-populated, this I would regard as a blessing rather than a problem. We have been given by history a brief breathing-space in which to raise living standards and develop our economy so that with luck we might avoid the unhappy fate of India, where raising of living standards is an insuperable problem because savings which could otherwise be used to increase capital per head are swallowed up in the battle to feed a rapidly multiplying population. When Africa's population explosion occurs, the problem will be continent-wide and call for united economic action. Now is the time for Africa's economic resources to be mobilised to prevent the creation of a great slum continent.

And what wealth Africa has locked away in the ground! Tentative geological surveys have already proved cobalt, radium, copper, diamonds, gold, manganese, vanadium, bauxite, coal, iron and tin. Many of these resources lie dormant because few states have the capital and skill to exploit them efficiently. Instead of piecemeal appeals for aid and isolated efforts, an overall strategy is urgently required so that costly duplication and reduplication can be avoided and loans raised on a much wider basis than the single State, whose credit-worthiness may be very limited. Many of our individual efforts to exploit this great wealth, though profitable in the short term, may prove to be robbery of the earth in the long run because we have not rationalised our efforts and treated some of these resources as reserves.

Pan-Africa is not for me a semi-mystical concept of unity. It is an economic necessity. But we must press ahead with our planning and negotiation immediately before our situation hardens and our economic resources are locked away in water-tight national compartments, to be opened and enjoyed only by those who happen to be standing over the place where this wealth is buried.

*   *   *

Realism demands that we face unflinchingly the enemies of African unity. Neo-colonialism, though often waved like a banner in the faces of the people by unscrupulous leaders to divert attention from their own short-comings, remains the greatest threat to Africa's unity. I understand the term to mean the attempt made by great powers to undermine the sovereignty of an African State by the use of subtle economic and political tools to replace the physical domination of the old colonialists. It is all too possible for an African country to emerge from the colonial prison to find itself enmeshed in a net of financial, diplomatic and ideological obligations which effectively destroy its freedom of action.

It is unlikely that any serious attempt will ever be made again to colonise parts of Africa by physical force—the alertness of the United Nations Organisation, the encouraging emergence of an international morality, the delicate balance achieved between the two giant nations, the United States and Soviet Russia, are all effective deterrents against a new invasion of Africa. But as the Bemba say, there are more ways of killing a leopard than the use of the spear. The manœuvrings of the Belgians to maintain control of the Katanga's copper, zinc, tin and uranium mines, the spider's web of financial links which still bind former French territories to the metropolitan power scream warnings to independent African States that though the colonial power has waned, the colonial instinct and motivation still persist.

Neo-colonialism takes many forms. Let me list some of them:

1. Maintaining the domination of foreign capital within the economy of the independent State and preventing the break-up of the old colonial structure of the economy, whereby the colony was the supplier of cheap raw materials and served as a closed market for the goods of the imperial power.

2. Inflicting upon an African state in the closing days of colonial domination such elaborate and sophisticated governmental and administrative institutions that dependence upon expatriate skills became inevitable after independence.

3. Maintaining strategic positions by the establishment of military bases.

4. Imposing upon a nation, too young and weak to resist, diplomatic and co-operation agreements which undermine its sovereignty.

5. The erection of tariff walls across the African continent through such international trade groupings as the European Economic Community, which must inhibit the rational development of an African economy by joining some African states to Europe and excluding others.

6. Inflaming tribal and personal rivalries destructive of national unity either through the imposition of an Independence Constitution which entrenches tribalism or racialism or by the outright buying of the loyalty of disgruntled elements within the State.

Many of the leaders of the newly independent African states found themselves in an impossible position on the morning after Independence. With the best will in the world, they could not hold up their heads as free men because they were abjectly dependent upon foreign aid to maintain the bare machinery of government. And the offer of aid for specific projects gently prodded them in a direction the donor nation wished them to move. It would be churlish to refuse to acknowledge the debt owed by Africa to the wealthier nations. But no doubt they will also understand a certain wariness inculcated in us over the years of colonial domination. The original colonial gift to Africa incurred obligations of servitude and robbed us of our manhood. History must not repeat itself.

Neo-colonialism is destructive of Africa's unity because it creates mutual suspicion amongst newly independent states. We find ourselves asking: is that truly the voice of a particular people speaking or is international finance or an imperial power speaking through them, luring us away from our goal for their own purposes? African unity is going to require considerable sacrifices from individual states. It will call for a degree of integrity from Africa's leaders whereby they are bound to ask before accepting links with blocs or powers outside the Continent—will this association, though demonstrably to the economic benefit of my own nation, hinder the cause of African unity and cut across basic African interests?

*　　　*　　　*

I also see the infiltration of foreign ideologies such as Marxist Communism as a threat to African unity. We are well aware that Africa, as the Uncommitted Continent, is the arena of a silent, unseen struggle. We know that both the great world power blocs would count it a rich prize to be able to recruit Africa to their side. We are equally adamant that Africa's destiny is to remain non-aligned. This non-alignment, as Dr Nkrumah has pointed out, is not neutrality. We intend to do no fence-sitting act in world affairs. We reserve the right to examine all international problems in the light of our Continent's interest and decide our policy without ideological commitment. Our role in world affairs is not to remain aloof from the basic human issues which have led to the creation of two power blocs, but to exercise our influence with both sides in order to cement understanding between them and testify to the universal desire for peace and fruitful co-existence.

The fear abroad amongst the imperial powers that Africa might move into the communist camp is partly a spectre of their own making. For it was long customary in the loose terminology of colonialism to group together as enemies of the colonial power, communists, nationalists, liberals and natural rebels indiscriminately. South Africa's Suppression of Communism Act is invoked with gay abandon against Conservative Afrikaans clergymen, African nationalists, violently anti-communist liberals such as Pat Duncan as well as against avowed Marxists. This foolish tendency of colonial powers to label all critics of the régime as communists has done more damage to the cause of the West than all the millions of money spent by the Eastern bloc on propaganda beamed upon Africa. It has given the term communism wide currency and has also stimulated a certain curiosity in more simple African minds about its nature and teachings. Some have reasoned thus: if the Colonial Government is so vehemently against communism, then there must be something in it for us!

There are a number of simple facts which ought to abate some of the hysteria which attaches to the communist bogey in Africa. In the first place, communism appears to have discovered Africa so late in the day that the liberation struggle was almost over before the ideological offensive upon the Continent got under way. Communism's appeal to subject peoples is first and foremost as a technique and instrument of liberation. But the communist offer of help in the freedom struggle was so belated that it was like throwing a lifebelt to a swimmer in difficulty just as he drags himself to shore. But by the same token, it should be recognised that it is not the peoples of independent African states who are likely to turn to the works of Karl Marx for solace so much as those languishing under white-dominated governments at the southern tip of the Continent. There is a real danger of the rigidity and repressions of the Rhodesian, South African and Portuguese régimes driving their subject peoples into the arms of the communists through sheer desperation. So when Mr Ian Smith claims to have prevented the seeping down of communism from the North by declaring U.D.I., he is demonstrating a political naïvety which is pathetic. Any Marxist theorist would be happy to give him an elementary lesson in the tactics of subversion and leave him in no doubt that it is repressive régimes which allow no political expression to large masses of their populations which provide the really fertile seed-beds for communism. Peoples who have won their freedom from the domination of London, Brussels or Paris are unlikely to place themselves willingly under the domination of Moscow or Peking.

I believe too, that nationalism has proved a more powerful force than communism in the twentieth century. Surely the conflict between Peking and Moscow, the Hungarian uprising (which was anti-Russian rather than anti-communist in orientation) and the independent stance of Yugoslavia all underline this truth. However effective the propaganda beamed upon Africa by the communist bloc, sooner or later they need a sizeable physical presence if they are to win over the Continent. The history of the handful of communist parties on the Continent has not been an impressive one. They have foundered upon the rocks of indigenous political ideologies such as nationalism or religious ones such as Islam. It is this element in nationalism I have mentioned before—the search for African Personality which maintains a strong grip upon the African people which no foreign ideology could dislodge. For this reason, even those African intellectuals who toy with Marxist ideas reject International Communism. Nowhere has this clash between African self-consciousness and the demands of communism been more eloquently expressed than by Aimé

Césaire's letter of resignation from the French Communist Party following the disclosure by Khruschev at the Twentieth Party Congress in 1956 of the misdeeds of Stalin:

. . . we coloured men, in this specific moment of historical evolution, have consciously grasped, and grasped in its full breadth, the notion of our peculiar uniqueness, the notion of just who we are and what, and that we are ready, on every plane and in every department, to assume the responsibilities which proceed from this coming into consciousness. The peculiarity of our place in the world is not to be confused with anyone else's. The peculiarity of our problems, which aren't to be reduced to subordinate forms of any other problem. The peculiarity of our history, laced with terrible misfortunes which belong to no other history. The peculiarity of our culture, which we intend to live and to make live in an ever realler manner.*

To shatter the myth of the all-pervasive influence of communism in Africa is not by any means to under-estimate its activity or its dangers. One estimate puts the number of communists on the African continent at a derisory 50,000 out of our 200 million people. But the strength of communism is not related to statistics. Each of those fifty thousand dedicated party members will be well-trained, utterly fanatic, strategically placed and totally convinced of the rightness of his beliefs. His influence will outweigh his isolation. Already we have seen a major communist success in ideological division of the labour movements of Africa. Communist agents have been fishing in the murky waters of the Congo situation. Nowhere in the world is there a bad state of affairs which communists will not endeavour to make worse. Of the two communist propaganda offences directed at Africa, that of the Chinese is the more effective because China has known the struggle against colonialism and the stigma of colour. Being an outcast from the United Nations, China is not bound by the niceties of diplomacy; the rules of

* Aimé Césaire, quoted by Legum, *Pan Africanism*. Pall Mall, 1962, p. 106.

international morality do not apply to her. For these reasons, her propaganda offensive is worthy of greater respect and calls for special vigilance.

Any success which the communist bloc may achieve in aligning African States with it is destructive of Africa's unity and causes a shift of loyalty from Pan-Africa to Pan-Communism. Ideological subservience must be seen for what it is—a subtle and debilitating form of colonial domination which can carve up Africa as effectively as anything achieved by the Great Powers in the late nineteenth entury.

*   *   *

Our discussion on the economic aspect of neo-colonialism prompts some thoughts on this whole question of aid for under-developed nations. Several distinguished economists have pointed out what we at the receiving end can confirm from our own experience, that the present situation with regard to outside aid is unsatisfactory, both in the sense that there is a fundamental lack of co-ordination and predictability about it, and also that the nations who receive it are not always either willing or able to make the best use of it.

I have read somewhere that foreign aid accounts for something like one-half of one per cent of the total income of rich countries, and it is clear that there is growing resistance amongst the voters of some of these nations to maintain, let alone increase, this level of giving. They point to the economic black spots in their own countries; the apparent churlish ingratitude of the receiving nations in not rewarding this largesse by more obvious ideological commitment to their foreign policy aims, and to the suspicion that it may be squandered by the inefficiency and incompetence of governments, whose shortcomings and set-backs are splashed across the headlines of their press but whose problems, not being regarded as 'hard news', do not warrant the big black type.

Some critics might claim that as the leader of a nation at

the receiving end of this economic assistance, it behoves me to accept gratefully what is given and to recognise that it is not my business to offer advice to those nations who provide it. This is of course the very root of the problem. In many circles, foreign aid is regarded as 'charity'—a collective version of the penny given to the beggar or the coin dropped into the collection box, and by definition charity is supposed to be unplanned, spontaneous and unbusinesslike. It also implies no commitment for the future. Its continuance depends upon the object of the charity engaging the sympathy of the donor.

From the receiver's point of view, the comparative unpredictability of foreign aid is a major difficulty. Newly independent States are actively engaged in planning two or three decades ahead; their development plans are detailed for at least five years. Their biggest challenges in the economic field cannot possibly be met in the short run. Hence we have a real sense of insecurity about the continuance of foreign aid. To what extent are we able to take into account in our planning the assurance that present grants will continue? Must we operate on the assumption that they are windfalls —to be accepted with gratitude but not incorporated into our long-term planning? I am of course aware of the political realities that govern foreign aid grants. Many legislatures vote annually their overseas funds to fit in with their normal budget presentation. Changes of government through the natural processes of democracy can also decisively affect policy towards aid for undeveloped countries. Every electoral reversal in a donor nation creates great anxiety in the governments of receiving countries. Will attitudes to overseas aid radically alter and will the redemption of electoral promises demand greater concentration upon domestic economies at our expense? Hence it is difficult to fulfil one of the main requirements for rational development planning—predictability of the sources and level of capital over a period of years.

Foreign aid also tends to be piecemeal and often tied to specific projects. The local representative of an international aid agency may have strong views on the economic priorities of the country in which he is resident. Once he succeeds in persuading his principals that his own predilections for a dam or a railway or an educational institution are justified, the funds which arrive will be committed to these projects alone, in isolation from the overall development plan which the government itself has evolved. The type of aid is also naturally related to what the donor nation can easily provide, so that the course of economic development in the poor nation is partly directed, not by the facts of the situation, but by the prodigality of certain resources in advanced countries.

At the present time, it is abundantly clear that aid does not always go to the countries who most need it. Donor nations have certain 'favourites' amongst the under-developed countries, either because of traditional links, or because their economic experts, understandably anxious to direct aid where the results will be most dramatic, tend to concentrate upon areas with great growth potential or where they know that adequate administrative machinery exists to apply it. But there are hopeless cases amongst the under-developed countries, where the administrative machinery to apply foreign aid does not exist, and where there is a real possibility that some of this precious transfusion of capital may be squandered or used unwisely. Surely the answer here is not to 'blacklist' the poor nations in such desperate straits, but to provide alongside the aid the professional and technical skills needed to train nationals to control it wisely.

Where then do the components of an answer to these critical problems lie? We must obviously get rid of the concept of foreign aid as a form of charity offered by the rich to the poor. This frankly calls for a thorough-going effort to educate the rich nations in the political realities of the modern world. Strategic interdependence is universally conceded, the next step is to demonstrate the economic inter-dependence of our one world. The obligation of the rich to help the poor is partly a matter of morality but can also be justified on the grounds of enlightened self-interest. The political instability which is a consequence of economic distress in the under-developed country has its effect in shrinking the market for the products of the advanced nation. Rationally applied economic aid is good business sense because it will provide scope for private investment and help create an ever-larger world market.

In strategic terms, there is no longer such a thing as a local war. Upheaval, revolution and dispute in small nations in the heart of the African or Asian continents can decisively affect the delicate balance of world power. Since economic distress is often an element in such local conflagrations, the rich nations may discover that they are required to spend many times more on the instruments of war to prepare for the escalation of these local conflicts, than they would need to help build the economic foundations of political stability on the spot.

Most important of all, there is need to institutionalise foreign aid so that it is taken as a *sine qua non* that a given percentage of the national income of an advanced nation is set aside for foreign aid programmes. This will avoid the need for the constant argument that attends the regular intro-duction of foreign aid bills in the legislature—debates which re-opens the basic question of the obligation or otherwise to help poor nations.

A scheme for the co-ordination of aid to under-developed nations from various sources is proposed by Dr Dudley Seers, the Director of the Economic Development Division of the United Nations Economic Commission for Africa, who in a stimulating paper* argues the points I have made above with much greater economic knowledge than I can command. This plan is worthy of the closest possible atten-

* 'International Aid—the Next Step', *Journal of Modern African Studies*, Vol. 2, No. 4.

tion both by the governments of donor nations and of under-developed countries. We must reach as rapidly as possible that point in the evolution of international morality and education where certain clear-cut aims can be dramatically spelled out as the very minimum that all the world owes to any part of it. Goals like world literacy, and the removal of health scourges such as malaria and bilharzia, are feasible in our lifetime if all the forces of goodwill can be marshalled and economic and technical aid put on a rational basis. But no amount of aid from outside the Continent can obscure the responsibility which Pan-Africa has towards its own critically affected members. Unless the under-developed nations of Africa are to have all their self-confidence eroded away, and become psychologically conditioned to being beggars parading their sores outside the palaces of the rich West, they must conjure with one simple fact—that no nation is so poor that it cannot do *something* for a neighbour in need. The offer of a handful of maize from a virtually empty storehouse, though derisory as a solution to a poor neighbour-nation's problem compared with the avalanche of aid from the West, is symbolic both of mature nationhood in the donor, and of an identification which will bode well for Africa's future unity.

*   *   *

It is a profitless exercise to try to predict the future shape of Africa, to describe the possible regional groupings between States which may be a jumping-off point for continental unity. Our nations are still dynamically evolving; in many areas national boundaries have not been defined beyond all possibility of dispute. But one of the great hindrances to accelerating the re-grouping of African nations should be mentioned. We are committed absolutely by our rejection of the methods of colonialism to any use of force in imposing new patterns upon Africa. I am not now referring to the liberation of the white-dominated

States in the south of the continent but to the suppression of small regional dissidents in free Africa. How much simpler it would be if the large and powerful nations, having agreed upon desirable groupings, could then impose their will by armed force upon certain small states or regions where fanatical xenophobia is practised, and who are impervious to all pleas that they should become reconciled to their neighbours in the interests of Pan-African unity. The coercion which has been used throughout history (sometimes in the best interests of those suffering it) to bring about large political groupings is not open to us. The old colonialists used force to define many of the boundaries of Africa. We are not prepared to use the same means to alter them. Closer links between nations must be voluntarily entered upon without outside pressures other than the power of persuasion and preaching of the Gospel of Unity.

At this point we must responsibly recognise that the force which created the new nations—nationalism—can work against the ultimate aim of African unity. The more successful we are in sharpening a people's consciousness of being a nation, the less likely they are to take kindly to submerging that new-found identity in a wider union. Africans would be less than human if they did not exult in their sense of ethnical identity after the long period of enforced anonymity under the colonialists. The late Sir Abubakar Tafawa Balewa expressed a widely held view when he roundly stated in 1960 'A United States of Africa? Surely it is premature to start talking about anything like this. Nigeria has not the slightest intention of surrendering her sovereignty, no sooner has she gained her independence, to anyone else. . . .' Such views must be respected, for we should remember that Africa as a continent is not a homogeneous 'supra-natural entity', arbitrarily divided within restricted boundaries. Because Africans happen to share a black skin it does not follow that national feeling is an illusion. The citizens of Europe happen to share white skins but suggestions that Berlin or Rome or

Paris should become the headquarters of a United States of Europe would find strong resistance in almost every country. Certainly we have to thank the colonialists for one thing—the emphasis upon the backwardness of those with black skins has, by a process of compensation, made 'Blackness' a real bond amongst Africans. But it is naïve to assume that independent African States would necessarily find it more congenial to have their sovereignty vested in Accra, Lagos, Nairobi or Lusaka than in London, Paris or Brussels as was the case in colonial days. Such facts must be faced squarely or all our attempts to unify Africa are bound to founder because we have ignored hard realities in our intoxication with fond illusions.

Certain guide-lines for advance can be distinguished which leave us little excuse for despair.

1. Closer links are being forced upon groups of states by the realities of international and continental politics. If I may be parochial, Zambia is in the process, as a matter of urgency, of extending her trade and communication links with the East African territories and reducing the dependence upon the white-dominated States of Southern Africa, forced on her in times past. We have at least Mr Ian Smith's illegal declaration of Rhodesian independence to thank for injecting urgency into the plans we were in process of formulating to provide new outlets to the sea in a northward direction, and the investigation of new sources of supply for the goods we had traditionally obtained from Rhodesia and South Africa. What we would have got around to doing anyway tomorrow, the pressure of political events has thrust to the head of today's agenda. Zambia's survival now inhibits us from looking inwards and concentrating upon domestic problems. International trade and communication have become urgent priorities in our national planning. We had always feared that the policies of white-dominated States might threaten our life-lines and place us in the impossible moral dilemma of helping inadvertently, for

reasons of economic dependence, to bolster régimes whose downfall we are committed to achieve. It is providential that our new state has not had time to structure her economy in such a way that her survival depends upon the continuance of such links. Now all our national planning must be based upon the establishment of closer ties with our independent neighbours, not as a desirable goal but an immediate necessity.

2. The existence of a Common Enemy in the shape of the Portuguese, South African and Rhodesian Governments is a great aid to Pan-African unity. We know that so long as millions of our brothers are denied basic human rights and political expression, we ourselves will never be truly free. The urge to free them has become the basis of a common African foreign policy. Many petty differences and squabbles amongst independent States fade into insignificance compared with the travail of fellow-Africans still in chains. These final strongholds of alien domination are an affront to Africa's integrity. We cannot rest whilst our comrades languish. Our enjoyment of our own freedom is soured by the knowledge of their sufferings. Pan-Africa cannot shunt her responsibilities on to the United Nations Organisation or the Great Powers, though in each case we feel that little more than lip-service is being paid by them to condemnation of repressive régimes. Much of our active planning is now taken up with ways and means of aiding the freedom struggle in these police-states. And because of our preoccupation with this great crusade, I am hopeful that many of the barriers to African unity represented by minor squabbles amongst the free nations will wither and die for lack of attention as the antagonists are forced to look outwards and recognise their true enemies.

3. We have a Charter for African unity in the document which emerged from the epoch-making Addis Ababa Summit Conference of African Heads of State. Because Zambia was not at that time a sovereign state, I was unable to add my

signature to that of the thirty Heads of State who signed it. But my Government heartily endorses both the letter and spirit of that Declaration and is prepared to work within it. Besides expressing a number of general sentiments concerning African unity, the blueprint was drawn for the setting up of machinery for closer co-operation—the first step towards that majestic concept, a United States of Africa.

I am aware that there are many cynics abroad who regard such charters as pieces of paper, couched in cliché and having no more binding force than a certain vacuous goodwill. Much the same was said, no doubt, about the Constitution of the United States of America when a group of visionaries assembled to draft it, having little in a concrete sense to confirm their hopes. The Charter of the United Nations Organisation has suffered similar vilification. But what body of international morality now exists has been consolidated and guided by that historic document. The Addis Ababa Charter, like every similar document, is a most potent force for achieving the large scale goals of the human race. It testifies to the fact that individual nations are prepared to place themselves under the goad of some larger good and acknowledge that they are not laws unto themselves. We are, thank God, reaching that stage of civilisation in the modern world that when we deliberately violate some constitution or charter which regulates relations between nations, we are aware that we have done so; we acknowledge the sovereignty of some higher law even in the breach of it.

But the Addis Ababa Charter did much more than testify to general principles. It laid down a larger number of specific courses of action concerning decolonisation, racial discrimination, non-alignment, general disarmament and economic problems. This Charter is more than a pious hope; it embodies a workable strategy and secretariat to direct it.

I am not naïve enough to presume that the cause of African unity will be a majestic progression along the lines laid down in the Charter, unhindered by dissension and setbacks. But just as the People of Israel, having been given the Law, then had to descend from the mountain top and march for many weary years through the wilderness before establishing a kingdom where that Law reigned supreme, so from the mountain top of Ethiopia, the nations of Pan-Africa will have to face the dangers of the desert way before their Law comes into its kingdom. But when all the weaknesses of such a Charter have been exposed, the honest man would have to admit that Africa has been able to find more common ground in the past two decades than Europe or any other continent has marked out in centuries. Would to God that every other continent were able to agree upon such specific common aims and policies. The cause of world peace and brotherhood would be immeasurably advanced.

4. The very richness and diversity of viewpoint on the African continent, whilst liable to fossilise into power-blocs with labels such as Monrovia or Casablanca, is paradoxically a powerful aid to unity. Were any one independent state utterly dominant over the Continent, then it would become a matter of honour for others to resist its influence and reject its ideas. But many nations have already contributed to the growing body of common policy. To Ghana we owe the first spelling out of the idea of a United States of Africa. Former French territories have outlined the concept of the African Personality and given it literary and artistic reality. The Sudan has been the prime mover in the demand for nuclear test bans on the African continent. 'Moderate' members of the African community such as Nigeria and Liberia can claim credit for schemes for modest but valuable economic and political co-operation. Pan-Africa is fertile of ideas, plans and policies which it is possible to consider on their merits. It is not necessary to have the loudest voice or the biggest army to have your views prevail. Every independent state has some gem, however small, to add to the treasury of Africa's ideological wealth, so that every State will some day be proud to point to some brick

in the foundations of Africa's unity which was their gift. Eventual unity will not be the result of the imposition of one dominating national personality but will result from dialogue amongst many, leading to a growing consensus to which political and economic shape can be given.

5. Africa is a young continent, not in terms of its belated discovery by the world in historical time, but in the literal sense that the vast majority of its peoples and leaders are youthful. In my own country, Zambia, over fifty per cent of our population is under the age of 20. Youth is characterised by idealism, enthusiasm and elasticity of mind. It is the rising generation whom we must imbue with the spirit of African unity. The young people of Africa are likely to have a more sophisticated outlook upon international affairs than their elders. Mercifully, too, many of the personal feuds which have disfigured the early Pan-African movement will perish of old age—leading figures who were involved in rivalry will pass from the scene. In this regard I heartily endorse the proposal made by His Imperial Majesty Haile Selassie, Emperor of Ethiopia, in his opening address to the Addis Ababa Summit Conference that there should be an African University sponsored by all African states where, in his own words 'the future leaders of Africa can be trained in an atmosphere of continental brotherhood. In this African institution, the supra-national aspects of African life would be emphasised and study would be directed toward the ultimate goal of complete African unity.' At all costs, our young men must be educated to see Africa whole and to see it steadily. No greater disservice could be done to the African cause than the implanting in young minds of seeds of suspicion of other states based upon matters of historical rivalry which must be buried for ever.

The superficial observer sees little to show for Pan-Africanism other than a profusion of committees, study groups, manifestos and public speeches with an internationalist flavour. On the other side of the balance he places the disquietening evidence of a state of affairs which seems to mirror the national conflicts and rivalries of Europe. I passionately believe, however, that the ideal of African unity will shortly take a giant step forward. It will move out of the realm where it is a talking point, a specialist study, an intellectualist preoccupation, the concern of a few pressure groups. When we reach the point where mass parties are prepared to make African unity a plank in their political platforms and tell the electorate frankly that they will do everything possible if returned to power to accelerate political integration between States, then the movement towards African unity will cease to be an intellectual exercise and be actively launched on the search for a mandate from the people.

*   *   *

One of the things which puzzles African nationalists from former French territories is the support and loyalty given by former British colonies to the Commonwealth. Surely, they claim, the timely transformation of the British Empire into a Commonwealth was a subtle move to ensure British influence in and domination over the territories she could no longer rule by direct means? Must not the existence of the Commonwealth, they ask, be a barrier to African unity, grouping independent states in such a way as to keep alive the memory of their colonial orientation and bringing to bear upon them the pressure of British and white Dominion diplomacy to guide their foreign policies into the same orbit as Britain's? In spite of such misgivings on the part of nationalists historically orientated towards metropolitan France there has been a great drive on the part of those members of the French Community associated with the so-called Brazzaville group to transform the French Community into something closely approximating to the Commonwealth. There is a growing awareness in Africa of the value of the Commonwealth link to those nations who are fortunate enough to belong to it. And in no sense do I see these 'autonomous communities, equal in status and in no way subordinate to one another in their domestic and external affairs', to quote the Westminster Statute of 1931, as being a threat to Africa's eventual unity.

The transformation of Britain's Empire into a friendly grouping of nations who voluntarily enter into a relationship which in no way hinders their freedom of action and thought may well prove to be the greatest monument to British adaptability and ingenuity. In taking the initiative of transforming her relationship towards those nations historically bound to her from one of dominance to one of fraternity, Britain, though unable to re-write history in order to put a more favourable gloss upon her old colonial policies, has certainly done much to allay the bitterness which otherwise would have been directed against her by the peoples she has finally released from tutelage. Indeed, I would go as far as to say that if, in the mysterious out-workings of Providence or fate, Zambia was destined to be colonised by a Western Power, then thank God it was the British!

There could be no one more robustly anti-colonialist than Dr Kwame Nkrumah, but he has expressed his loyalty to the Commonwealth in the following words: 'States emerging from the tutelage of other colonial powers have not always understood Ghana's attachment to the Commonwealth. That is because the loose, *ad hoc* nature of the structure is not correctly comprehended by those who are members of more formal associations. It is difficult for those not accustomed to a *free* connection with Europe to appreciate that the Commonwealth is an association of sovereign states, each of which is free from interference from the others, including the United Kingdom.'*

The Commonwealth *is* an amazing association! Its uniqueness lies in the absence of compulsion upon any nation either to join it or remain in it, and the absolute equality

* K. Nkrumah, *Africa Must Unite* (New York: Praeger, 1963), p. 185.

amongst its members. The State which created one of the greatest Empires the world has ever known and the smallest, poorest nation are equal partners. Their votes are of equal value; their voices are listened to with the same attention. A miracle of forebearance and patience occurs at every Commonwealth meeting. These strange, invisible links prove strong enough to withstand the abhorrence which one member may feel for the policies of another. Some of the policies of the African States are anathema to the British way of life. Some of Britain's traditional alliances are with nations who are the mortal enemies of African freedom. Yet the links hold. Traditional allegiance to the Crown is often quoted as the cement which holds together the Commonwealth units. Without under-valuing the sentiment which attaches to this tradition-rich symbolism, my own view would be that responsible Commonwealth leaders find in the challenge to live in amity with other members from whom they differ radically in foreign or domestic policy a minuscule version of the ultimate challenge—the possibility of world government. Our feeling is that unless we can grow in community with nations whose attachments are grounded in the same tradition of British tutelage, there is little hope of an accommodation on a world scale being achieved. When serious attempts are made to create the first tentative structures of world government, it is the Commonwealth which will have most to contribute by way of experience and knowledge.

There are those who feel that the multiplicity of associations which a nation like Zambia contracts—O.A.U., the Commonwealth, the U.N.—are wasteful of our national resources and the time of our leaders. My own view is that it is through our membership of such international groupings that we shall achieve maturity in our approach to world affairs. For every such association puts strains upon our loyalty, forces us to formulate and enunciate our views on a thousand and one issues and teaches us the art of compromise by thrusting us into encounter with nations whose policies are uncongenial to us and with whom we have little direct contact.

But a word of warning is in order here. Whilst we smaller and more recent members gladly acknowledge the moral leadership of the United Kingdom in the counsels of the Commonwealth, there are issues of paramount importance to the free nations of Africa which could undermine Britain's leadership in our eyes. U.D.I. is one of them. There is growing suspicion that Britain's lack of resolution in bringing down the Smith Government is due to a sense of kinship with white Rhodesians which apparently does not extend to those with black skins and which is a denial of the non-racial basis of the Commonwealth. There are other grounds for suspicion in her cleaving to her 'oldest ally' Portugal as part of N.A.T.O., and her reluctance to damage her economic interests in South Africa by taking a more rigorous line in such matters as economic boycott and sanctions. On the horizon, too, looms another challenge of recent origin, the growth of racial discrimination within British society. Britain can lead the Commonwealth by moral influence along paths which will enrich every member only if her *bona fides* on the issue of racial equality is beyond reproach. There can be no compromise as far as the independent States of Africa are concerned on the issues of smashing the residual racist régimes on the Continent and freeing millions of Africa from the scourge of white domination. Whilst such issues as Britain's entry into the European Economic Community will create tensions within the Commonwealth, any lack of resolution in facing the racial issue will shatter it and force its African members to pursue alone or in new alliances their crusade to free the entire Continent.

*   *   *

The leaders of free Africa have spoken eloquently of their concern to unify the Continent in the Preamble to the

Declaration issued by the Addis Ababa Summit Conference. I quote:

We, the Heads of African States and Governments assembled in the city of Addis Ababa, Ethiopia, [are] . . .

. . . convinced that it is the inalienable right of all people to control their own destiny;

. . . conscious of the fact that freedom, equality, justice and dignity are essential objectives for the achievement of the legitimate aspirations of the African peoples;

. . . conscious of our responsibility to harness the natural and human resources of our continent for the total advancement of our peoples in spheres of common endeavour;

. . . inspired by a common determination to strengthen understanding and co-operation amongst our states in response to the aspirations of our peoples for brotherhood and solidarity, in a large unity transcending ethnic and national differences;

. . . convinced that, in order to translate this determination into a dynamic force in the cause of human progress, conditions for peace and security must be established and maintained;

. . . determined to safeguard and consolidate the hard-won independence as well as the sovereignty and territorial integrity of our states and to fight against neo-colonialism in all its forms;

. . . dedicated to the general progress of Africa;

. . . persuaded that the Charter of the United Nations and the Universal Declaration of Human Rights, to the principles of which we reaffirm our adherence, provide a solid foundation for peaceful and positive co-operation among states; and

. . . resolved to reinforce the links between our states by establishing and strengthening common institutions . . . .

A programme to keep us busy for quite a while!